The Voyage of the Rose City

SPIEGEL & GRAU · *New York* · 2011

The Voyage of the

ROSE CITY

An Adventure at Sea

JOHN MOYNIHAN

ILLUSTRATIONS BY THE AUTHOR

The Voyage of the Rose City is a work of nonfiction. Some names and identifying details have been changed.

Published in the United States by Spiegel & Grau, an imprint of The Random House Publishing Group, a division of Random House, Inc., New York.

SPIEGEL & GRAU and Design is a registered trademark of Random House, Inc.

All photographs, unless otherwise credited, are from the personal collection of John Moynihan.

LIBRARY OF CONGRESS CATALOGING-IN-PUBLICATION DATA

Moynihan, John McCloskey
The voyage of the Rose City / John Moynihan.
p. cm.
ISBN 978-0-8129-8243-5
eBook ISBN 978-0-679-64381-4
1. Moynihan, John McCloskey—Travel. 2. Merchant mariners—United States—Biography. 3. Seafaring life. 4. Rose City (Oil tanker) I. Title.
VK140.M69A3 2011 387.5092—dc22 2010052485 [B]

Printed in the United States of America on acid-free paper

www.spiegelandgrau.com

9 8 7 6 5 4 3 2 1

FIRST EDITION

Book design by Simon M. Sullivan

Dedicated to the crew of the *Rose City*

"When I was a boy with never a crack in my heart."
—W. B. YEATS, "The Meditation of the Old Fisherman"

PREFACE
by Elizabeth Moynihan

JOHN HAD A GREAT WANDERLUST, which, I admit, I encouraged. But during spring break from Wesleyan in 1980, when John told us he would like to "ship out" in the Merchant Marine for the summer, his father and I had vastly different views of such an adventure. Pat was in his first term as United States Senator, but when he was John's age he had worked on the New York City docks, then joined the Navy, and he cautioned that it might be a tough experience. But as a passionate former sailor, I was excited that John might sail across the equator or circle the globe, so I immediately set about helping him. In the middle of the night on the date he was set to sail, he phoned us from a deserted New Jersey dock with the alarming news that the ship was not there. As we talked, a car arrived, crew members spilled out, and he hurried off.

Following his voyage, John spent the spring semester at Trinity College, Dublin, and then returned to Wesleyan in the autumn. He was accepted into Paul Horgan's writing tutorial, which required students to produce a book. He hoped the journal he'd kept while aboard the *Rose City* could serve as the basis of one, a proposal Mr. Horgan accepted. Although John spent much time thinking through the process, by term's end

John Moynihan on the *Rose City*

he had produced only a brief outline and a few sample pages for Mr. Horgan's review, leaving the disappointed tutor with no choice—he'd have to drop John from the course. At their first meeting in the new term, when Paul Horgan unhappily raised the subject of the book, John stopped him by holding up 270 typewritten pages and asking, "This book?" He had spent the entire month-long break holed up in his room, writing. Mr. Horgan was pleased with his effort and suggested, with the comment, "Keep sailing—you're on your way," that John work on a second draft for the university honors program. He received his degree with High Honors in General Scholarship.

Pat was proud of John for making the most of the voyage and writing the journal; he loved *The Voyage of the Rose City* and hoped it would be published. But when I tried to read it I was appalled—how could I have put my child at such risk?

His life had been in danger—not once but repeatedly! I was so upset and consumed by guilt I couldn't read it.

Pat retired from the Senate in January 2001 and died in March of 2003; then, the following year, John died from a fatal reaction to acetaminophen. In 2006, two years after John's death, when I was still sorting through his papers and possessions, I finally read *The Voyage of the Rose City*. I was deeply moved, and so impressed by what he knew about people, the world, and himself when he was barely twenty. For almost two years I kept going back to John's journal in my despair over his death. He was a wonderful son, a high-spirited, talented fellow who died suddenly just when he was about to start a new life in Australia.

John's voyage on the *Rose City* was the most powerful and formative experience in his life, and his account of it reflects his spirit, intelligence, and heart. I felt compelled to publish a limited edition of *The Voyage of the Rose City* to preserve and share it. It was a healing experience to take the pages of his loose-leaf notebook and drawings from his sketchbook and turn them into a book. Working with Stoneroot Industries, compositors in Stamford, New York, near the farm Pat and I had for almost forty years, was restorative.

I had one hundred copies printed, and on June 26, 2010, the anniversary of the date the *Rose City* sailed across the equator, John's brother and sister and I had a publication party with about fifty family friends. It was also the night of the June full moon. John and I called ourselves "moon freaks" because wherever we were in the world, when the moon was full we would try to find each other and talk. It was a curious and delightful

bond; I say it's due to his having been born on Galileo's birthday.

Shortly after this, Celina Spiegel heard about the book and
called to ask if she could read it. She liked it! I am thrilled that
John's account of his experience on a supertanker can be shared
with a wider public and live on. I am grateful to Spiegel &
Grau for making this possible.

Part I

YOU'RE NOT
PAID TO THINK!

CHAPTER 1

THE CALL CAME IN AT MIDNIGHT. One of the 12–4 watch
banged on my door and gave me the word: all hands on
deck to let go in forty minutes. Within fifteen the crew had assembled in the lounge on A deck. The Bosun shuttled back and
forth between the bridge and the main deck, straightening out
the logistics and trying to encourage a crew that was already
tired and restless. This was it—within a couple of hours, all
twenty-seven of the current crew of the SS *Rose City* would be
committed to an overseas voyage, and only the executive board
of the company sitting in the bidding room in Seattle could
really say for how long.

The 8–12 and 12–4 watches disappeared down the aft stairway to work the stern. The 4–8 watch (Billy, Jake, and me) and
the Bosun shuffled down the main passageway and headed for
the bow. The quarter-mile walk from the house to the bow took
about five minutes. Along the way Billy and Jake briefed me on
the job that lay ahead. More important, they told me how to
write it up on the overtime sheet. "Every minute counts. Take
'em for all you can get. Snatch it up!" Jake would say, grabbing
as if to lift J. Paul Getty's wallet.

Waiting for us on the bow was the chief mate, a tall, overweight man who wielded his walkie-talkie for all the command it could garner him. He and the Bosun conferred in authoritative tones at one end of the foredeck while Billy, Jake, and I leaned against the port anchor block, waiting to begin hauling in the five-inch-thick sea lines that trailed down from the gypsy heads to the docks below. Billy began to complain. Jake reacted by breaking into one of his comic monologues and cracking Billy up. Then the word came in from the bridge over the Chief's radio, causing Billy to immediately affect an air of gravity. The Bosun mounted his short, fat frame before the winch controls and Jake took position nearby, working the lines on the winch roller. Such is the prerogative of old-timers. Billy and I grabbed the lead line and stood by. Below, on the dock, one of the longshoremen cast off the first line, and the Bosun threw on the winch. I followed Billy's motions, dragging the line across the deck and folding it into neat lines along the starboard rail. The sea-soaked and brine-encrusted line grew heavier and heavier as we got to the end that lay in the water by the pier. As the eye of the line was pulled up, Jake yelled at me to help Billy, who was dragging the last twenty feet across the deck by himself. "Always back a man up!" This was my first on-hand lesson in the empathy among seamen. I grabbed the tail end and helped Billy stow it with the rest of the line.

By the fourth line my arms were dead. The winch only pulled the lines onto the deck; we had to stow them away. But gradually a rhythm set in. Jake and the Bosun set the pace, Billy and I executed it. The Chief leaned against the bulkhead and watched. The Bosun was uncharacteristically quiet around the Chief, and the other two wordlessly obeyed his commands.

On the other hand, the Chief was continually glancing up at the bridge, where he knew the Captain stood watching. How the body politic functioned for the rest of the crew was as yet unknown to me. I had but one concern: to shut up and watch what the others did and try to learn it all as quickly as possible. It wasn't exactly the First Law of the Jungle, but the stakes were just as high.

The stern was the first part of the ship to be free of the dock, much to the chagrin of the 4–8 watch, which always had to work the bow. The stern not only has fewer lines than the bow, but it is also worked by both the 8–12 and the 12–4 watches. Just deserts, as it turned out: The 4–8 watch gets three more hours of overtime than the other two.

The port spring line was the last to go. The Chief, clutching his radio, stared at the dockworkers below. They weren't going to sea. As we let go, they'd leave for home; that was the unspoken thought in everybody's mind.

The Bosun had been primarily concerned throughout the night only with the job at hand: Get the crew working, and don't get into a beef with the Chief. Billy and Jake just did the work, trying not to think about leaving. This was going to be a long voyage. The Chief's radio crackled: Let go the port spring line. For the last time the dockhand pulled the eye off the gypsy head and let it drop into the water. The Chief signaled the Bosun to start up the winch, and immediately our ears were pierced with the maddening whine of the outdated machinery grinding against itself. By now, neither Billy nor Jake had to yell out instructions above the roar—I responded automatically. The Bosun stared through his thick-lensed glasses at some undefined point beyond the bow. The Chief fidgeted with his radio and, with one eye on the bridge, surveyed our progress with a critical glare. Jake continued working the line on the winch, keeping up a truly magnificent semblance of hard work. Billy and I dragged the line. After a good five minutes the eye of the line finally slopped through the cholk, and the Bosun shut off the winch. It was now 2:30 a.m. The purring tugboats that eased us away from the docks would do all the work from here on out. With overtime money stashed safely away in our thoughts, we walked back to the house to catch an hour's sleep before we had to go on watch at 4:00 a.m. We had missed setting sail on Friday the thirteenth by two and a half hours. No one said anything on the walk back. Everyone was tired. Tired and committed.

By the time we were in the house and had climbed the two flights to B deck, where the crew cabins lay, the ship was sailing under her own power. The dark banks of the New Jersey shore slipped by with increasing rapidity. On deck one could hear the huge engine room, buried stories beneath the main deck, begin to hum. The entire ship started to vibrate with the awesome gyrations of the massive diesel engines that turned the two-story-high screw. While you sat in your cabin, lights off and a watch pending, the hugeness of the ship could swallow you whole.

chug chug chug

CHAPTER 2

I T WAS SIMPLY A QUESTION OF ESCAPE. Life at the university had become so unbearably entrenched that the only thing that mattered was getting as far away as possible. Something motivated me toward the Seafarers International Union to get my Z-card and a job out at sea.

Despite the sick feeling in my gut, that twinge every hitch-hiker knows between the time he decides to hit the road and is actually liberated by a series of rides, I felt optimistic and recklessly carefree.

Oddly enough, it was my parents who had helped me join the Merchants. As both a politician and former longshoreman, my father had a number of connections in the Seafarers International Union. Connections like that had helped a couple of my friends get jobs on freighters. This dream of a trip to any number of exotic lands, especially via so romantic and potentially lucrative a mode as the Merchant Marine, helped me to survive the last few manic days of the semester. It was in wonderfully ignorant bliss that I first became aware of the seaman's world.

At the union hall my contact, George, smiled when he arrived,

shaking my hand and dropping a few pleasantries. He knew I didn't belong in the SIU—any one of the cigarette-smoking idlers outside watching the call board could tell you that. But inside the organization, business is business. The union officials never talk outright; they speak with their whole bodies, letting out a few exclamations here and there to make their point. It is a nonverbal dialect that allows for discreet understandings between parties and prevents unwanted ears from listening in.

In this way George straightened me out on the logistics that go with obtaining Seaman's Papers. The first order of business was going to the Coast Guard station at Battery Park and presenting them with his letter assuring me work on a ship.

The Coast Guard station was classic Art Deco, sightly and genteel, a contrast with the attitudes of those inside waiting to get their Seaman's Papers. The half dozen or so drifters who sat in the waiting room sucking on their cigarettes were much like their counterparts in the union hall.

Many were ex-navy men, old vets who had yet to settle down

following their discharge, or who couldn't adjust to civilian life. I sat among them and smoked the better part of a pack myself. Periodically a gaunt kid in his twenties would call one of us behind the counter for the paperwork. The afternoon passed slowly.

At last it was my turn. The kid gave me a stack of forms to fill in, and I gave him my Social Security card. Then a large black woman fingerprinted me and told me to raise my right hand and repeat after her. The next thing I knew I had been sworn into the Coast Guard as a Merchant Marine.

With papers in hand, seabag packed, and a valid passport, I returned to the union hall. George was no longer involved in the process of shipping me out; Abe, the bureaucrat at the desk, had been left with instructions that I was to be "taken care of." He took me into the main office and sat me before a desk while he left to arrange my job. I looked around, amazed. There in the office was the most disparate collection of journeymen I'd seen on three continents. A Rastafarian hustling his way into a flyout job in Costa Rica. A lithe secretary scolding a 330-pound bosun for improper registration procedure. Labor officials laughing with swarthy gentlemen in dark suits.

Abe returned with my job ticket.

"Ordinary Seaman on the *Rose City*. Leaves from Camden, New Jersey, early tomorrow for forty-five days in the Mediterranean."

I inspected the job ticket and felt a thrill of butterflies run up my spine.

Abe gave me a hard look. "You're John Moynihan. So far as anybody's concerned, your father is a bartender on the West Side."

I smiled. "He was, you know."

"I know. Good luck." We shook hands and I walked out accompanied by the furtive side-glances of those in the room.

That night I made my way to the Texaco refinery at Eagle Point in Camden. I got there at one a.m. and walked out to the empty pier where the ship was supposed to be. Somehow I'd imagined she'd be there already, friendly crewmen ready to greet me with a warm bunk and a cup of coffee. Instead there was only the hiss of the massive refinery, and the cold. Around three a.m. a security guard found me huddled over a hot-air vent for warmth and told me I could crash in the office. The office was locked, but the hall floor was warmer than the wet ground outside.

The dawn came and went, leaving the refinery looking like a madman's Erector Set creation in the harsh New Jersey sun. I sat on a bench outside the office, smoking my last pack of cigarettes between catnaps. Eventually a few taxis deposited other seamen at the gate. They had nothing to say, either to me or to one another. They only wanted to get on the ship before they changed their minds.

Then an old '67 Plymouth station wagon pulled up with eight noisy celebrants inside. They spilled out onto the pavement, took one look around, and, seeing that the ship wasn't there, jumped back into the car to the battle cry "To a bar! To a bar!"

When the dust settled, the other stranded seamen and I went back to the business of killing time. Before long two vans pulled up, followed by a caravan of cars. I nervously gravitated to where they set up shop, and soon found myself drinking dollar beers with a couple of the boys.

The topic of conversation was why the ship was so late. This was soon learned, with the flash of police lights along the river. A huge Wagoneer roared across the grass and pulled up in front of the vans. One of the two passengers yelled to a buddy of his by the beer cooler that the cook had gotten into a knife fight with the steward and the cops weren't going to release the ship for another couple of hours.

People were generally surprised to hear about the delay, but not the fight. One fellow leaned over to me and said he'd been on a ship in South America. "Pirates climbed up the anchor chain and stabbed the man on watch thirty-seven times in the back." He chuckled. "The poor sucker didn't die." I drained my beer and reached for another.

The ship did arrive that morning, though. She glided up the river, one huge, magnificent envelope of steel. Moving at a nearly imperceptible pace, the huge bulk cautioned into the dock. I could make out on the bow the distant figures of men scrambling madly, desperate to finish their final chore and get the hell off the ship they had been stuck on for the past four months. As I stood amid the vast wasteland of the Texaco re-finery, the extent of the undertaking to which I was now committed was lost on me.

Up the long pier we walked. And with every step the ship grew in size. As we stood gathered next to her, waiting for the gangway to be lowered, the ship became disproportionately large, stretching the laws of physics to impossible limits. Then, looking around, I noticed a silent, angry fellow staring back at the shore. I thought he was just one of the boys, but something about him was different. Then he turned and began to question me in quiet, suspicious tones.

"What's your job? Where'd you get it? What time'd it go up on the board?"

I had no idea what he was talking about, or what the story was. I *did* know that somehow I was in trouble; the ordinary's job Abe got me in the New York City hall was meant for someone else.

I tried to bluff, acting nonchalant, as if I'd gotten the job by conventional means (even though at the time I hadn't a clue how a regular seaman got a job). He knew better. He was Billy Mahoney.

Standing on the port wing, watching the night grow slowly lighter, I recalled the scene as in a fitful dream, when unpleasant memories rise to the surface. Inside the bridge Billy continued to pace back and forth. The orange glow of his cigarette arched smoothly from his side to his mouth in rhythm with his step.

When I had made my way to my cabin on that first day at Eagle Point, the Chief told me to report to the Old Man. I climbed the stairwell to his office and presented him with my job ticket. He was a cagey old lifer who smoked rancid cigars out of a stubby brown holder he'd customized and barked out orders in a severe New York accent.

Before I'd even been in his office five minutes he asked me if I was related to Senator Moynihan. Caught off guard, I confessed I was. Then I realized that Abe back at the union hall knew what he was talking about: In the space of three seconds my status among the officers was drastically and permanently changed. The question was if, or rather when, the word would spread to the crew. That was an albatross I began to seriously dread. Billy knew something was very wrong with my story. He didn't know what, but he was sure as hell going to find out.

Chapter 3

T HE WATCH CALL CAME IN AT 3:20. Again one of the 12–4 watch broke my sleep. Routinely he informed me of the essentials: (a) It was 3:20 a.m.; (b) we were still going down-river, so the lookout would be on the bow instead of on the bridge; and (c) the weather was mild but I might need a light jacket. I flicked on the light by my bunk and rolled over. The watchman closed my door and moved on through the corridors to wake the rest of the 4–8.

Ten minutes later, Jake, Billy, and I had made it down to A deck and took coffee in the lounge. There Billy assumed position on one of the two sofas. Sitting at the coffee table by the door, I drank my mug of coffee and smoked one of my last Djarums. Billy squinted and jerked his head toward me. "What the fuck is that you're smoking?"

I explained that it was a Djarum, an Indonesian cigarette flavored with cloves, and as such discharged a distinctive, and lasting, scent. He sucked on his Marlboro and gave me the hairy eyeball. After a couple of minutes of silence he leaned back in his chair and let out a long stream of smoke before turning to me again.

"Well, I don't know about you, Monahan, but I'll give you a try." He almost smirked as he said it, his eyes again asquint, his mouth pulled back in a sardonic grimace. His tone was belligerent, but that is simply the way of the sea. He was beginning to know me for what I was: a skinny college kid who had snaked his way into a job. He was also letting me know straight out that he was itching for a fight. He looked away angrily and lit another cigarette. He wanted to know how I'd managed to get on a Philly ship from the New York hall. His buddy Ned had missed out on the Ordinary Seaman's job that I had and was now forced to work as maintenance-utility in the Steward's Department. Another of Billy's buddies who had been sitting in the Philly hall for two months waiting on a job had also missed out—all because a kid from New York managed to get one of the two available ordinary jobs before the ship even hit the boards in Philly. So he just kept looking away angrily and sucking on his cigarette.

There were only a few minutes left before we had to go on watch, so I grabbed a third cup of coffee. Jake left for the bridge, to go work the wheel. Billy lit up a final smoke before leaving to stand lookout on the bow. Because I didn't know how to work the wheel I had to stand by to relieve Billy and stand an extra-long lookout. Billy turned to me again and in his angry way said, "First thing you gotta learn, Monahan, is that a whore is a seaman's best friend; they take care of each other." Clint Eastwood could not have matched his final angry squint and grim half-smile as he got up and walked out to go on watch.

The lounge was a fair-sized room with a couple of couches, a few tables, and a library of forgotten books. Everything was metal and plastic. The tables all had half-inch lips around them so our mugs wouldn't slide off when the ship rolled at sea. And everything was bolted to the floor. I had about forty minutes to kill before I had to relieve Billy. The engines below occasionally roared louder and sent shudders through the eight-story super-structure of the house. Other than that, the only noise was the electric burning of the synchronized clocks that were mounted in every room on A deck. I read *The Log,* the Seafarers International Union (SIU) monthly paper, until Billy returned.

"The Chief wants you on the bow. The radio's out there by the rail. Just call in when you see a ship or a light." That was all he had to say. He sat down and immediately reached for another smoke. I walked onto the deck feeling more than a little confused. My primal fears started to prey on me and I was suddenly seized with dread halfway down the deck. Was it to the bow he wanted me to go? Maybe it was the bridge? Which end was the bow? Panicking, I ran back to the house and up the stairs to the lounge. Billy looked up in amazement. "What the hell are you doing here? You'd better get out on the bow before the Chief calls up on the radio!" I let out a string of nonsense in a feeble attempt to cover up my ignorance and idiocy. Billy threw another Squint of Death at me. "You know where the bow is, don't you?" I ran back down the stairs and out onto the bow.

It was lights-out on deck while the ship navigated the river channel. I fruitlessly groped for the radio in the dark, think-ing it was mounted on the railing. Finally I realized he meant the walkie-talkie that was sitting on one of the forward gypsy heads. The wind rushed up and blasted the forepeak; the mas-sive bulk of the ship churned up huge banks of water and cut through them with its iron edge. Farther downriver a glimmer of crimson—the lighted buoys—marked the dark river like lines on a highway. Several ships passed by, moving inland. Several more, the SS *Rose City* among them, headed into the rising sun and out to sea.

Weekends are money in the bank to a seaman. Unlike the selfless sailors of yesterday, the brothers of the SIU do not take in a gross percentage of the net profit; the modern sailor works a forty-hour week. In two four-hour shifts the seaman's watch comprises the average eight-hour workday, and for five days he gets nothing but a flat salary, unless he works overtime. But on the weekend even his watches pull in double time. Thus it was with minimal complaints that the crew of the *Rose City* turned to at eight in the morning on the first full day at sea.

I had been knocked off lookout at about 6:30 a.m. and walked back along the massive array of pipes that dominated the deck from the bow to the house. When I reached the lounge, Jake, who had been relieved at the wheel by Billy, told me to wake up both the 8–12 and the 12–4 watches at 7:20. It seemed the Chief had called all hands to secure the deck. Jake had made the Steward's Department coffee at six and given them a rouse shortly thereafter, so by the time I grabbed a cup of coffee they had drifted down to A deck.

The steward himself was a slow-paced old-timer, and the only black man on the ship. Insisting he be awakened an hour earlier than the rest of the Steward's Department, he would disappear into the mess and fiddle with the various breakfast preparations. The next to make his way down was, generally, Pete. He had been the first person I'd met on the pier as we waited for the ship to come in. He appeared a congenial enough fellow, despite his redneck haircut and caustic manner. As it turned out, he too was a college kid who had used connections to get on the ship. There was a great difference between his lot and my own, however. First, he had shipped out before, for the last two or three summers. More important, he was maintenance-utility, or, in other words, the cabin boy, the least desirable job on the ship. After dishing out the meals and swabbing the officers' mess, he had to go up to the C and D decks to make the officers' bunks and clean their toilets. He never had much to say when he came down; he just sat on the sofa with his coffee, a preppy non sequitur.

Then Miguel, the cook, would come up onstage. We would hear him from three rooms away, his maniacal laughter echoing off the bulkheads. The only holdover from the previous crew, this frenetic little Mexican had already established himself as the ship's trickster. He had risen from the poverty of Mexico City as a boxer, working alternately for the pre-Castro regime in Cuba and their stateside colleagues. Playing the eternal jester, he would go on at great length about his checkered boxing career. He even carried a .33 slug in his left side, a memento of an incident with an angry husband that left him officially declared dead before he finally pulled out of it.

Finally Ned would show up. Ned was not one to speak lightly, unless he was happily drunk. He arrived in the lounge that morning silent as usual. He had a singular appearance—his jack-tar physique lent him a knowing swagger, one he must have picked up from his days in the navy. He had a sharp crew cut and a single eyebrow that ran in a rigid, bushy line across the middle of his forehead. The way Ned sat down was an art in itself. First he would select his chair upon entering the lounge and then coolly saunter over to it. Once in position before his designated seat, in one fluid motion he would slip his hands into his pockets and, rolling his dark, sullen eyes back in his head, slink down into the seat while pulling out his pack of Kools. Before one realized, he had already lit the cigarette, now in the corner of his mouth, and tossed the pack on the table with a master prestidigitator's touch.

Time passed slowly on watch. Even when we were on standby and could sit in the lounge we were still on edge. The Chief could call up from the bridge at any moment and have us run the flag off the stern or perform some equally tedious duty. And there was always the fear of blowing it by oversleeping or forgetting to make a fresh pot of coffee for the next watch.

Eventually the time came to make my rounds. I went up to B deck and woke the Bosun first. He had a slightly larger cabin than the rest of the crew, and a private bathroom. Flicking on the overhead, I reported that the Chief had called all hands. He jerked himself up and swung his legs over the side of the bed. To see him dressed only in his briefs, it was clear how the years had worn down his five-foot-seven, two-hundred-plus-pound frame. An ex-boxer from South Philadelphia, he had brawled, balled, and caroused in every seaport imaginable. On his pudgy yet powerful arms were aquamarine tattoos of Popeye, Betty Boop, and various dancing girls that he had picked up in Pearl Harbor, back in '45. He rubbed his face and, putting on his half-inch-thick glasses, thanked me.

The two of the 8–12 watch lived in the two cabins across from the Bosun. I woke Tony first, banging on his door and stepping into his room to call all hands. He had been on the previous voyage, so his room was elaborately set up. Everything was secured by at least two or three ropes: his stereo, refrigerator, and plants. In his closet he kept a traveling wine cellar with a log in which he saved the labels and recorded all the wines he had picked up so far on the voyage. Even though he tried to look like your average seaman, at six-five and 220 pounds, he was distinctly different from the rest of the crew. He never joined the group in the lounge when we had a coffee break; instead he would slip up into his room and smoke his custom tobacco out of one of his many fine pipes. When Tony heard the call he lifted his head painfully from the pillow and nodded acknowledgment.

Next door was Peanuts, another old-timer, with more than twenty years sea time; in other words, since World War II he had spent twenty years actually at sea, the requirement for union pension. He had nothing to say when I woke him—he just uttered an unpleasant growl.

After that I woke the 12–4 watch: Bud, Jimmy, and Joe, the only other ordinary. The rest of the crew were qualified ABs (able-bodied seamen) who not only were more responsible for the operation of the ship but also earned a good deal more money. Joe was what they called a professional ordinary. An old-timer, he either never quite got around to upgrading himself or, as some of the crew thought, never bothered to, not wanting the extra responsibilities of an AB. He and I shared a bathroom and a very thin wall, so I often heard him shooting the breeze with one or another of the crew.

Bud and Jimmy, like Billy and Ned, were both in their mid-twenties. Philly boys like everyone else, they had both taken to the sea for lack of a better alternative. Bud was a severe character, his perfect body highlighted with a grim Aryan face and curly hair. Jimmy, on the other hand, was a potbellied, congenial fellow who refused to work extra overtime and made a point of sleeping as much as possible.

With everyone now called, I went back down to the lounge and waited for breakfast. Each morning the steward would post the day's menu, typed on his toy typewriter, announcing such culinary delights as Oxtail Soup and Fresh Frozen Milk. For the time being, no one had any real complaints about the food. Miguel did the best he could with what he had and, all in all, the *Rose City* was a pretty good feeder.

Every now and then one of the QMEDs (qualified members of the Engine Department) would show up in the lounge during watch. Because the ship's engines were so completely automated, it took only two people at a time—a QMED and an engineer—to run them. Thus there were only three members of the crew who worked down below—one for each watch. The only other member of the "black gang" was the pumpman, a small, wiry Indonesian who spoke broken English. The QMEDs were the old-timer Frank, perhaps the fattest human being alive, and two young fellows, Charlie and Matt.

It was a very tight crew. Just about everyone was from Philly, and they all knew one another, or had someone in common. In the mess, the old-timers would congregate around one table, and the boys, led by Billy, around another. The third table was neutral, generally occupied by the non-Philadelphians or latecomers. Already by the first morning at sea there was a developing polarization of the crew, each alliance hostile to the next but none overtly so. Like animals who take a direct stare

25" ayg, to Dwell OR not To Dwell
upon this Conical Nature...

all has become Silver on osaka harbour, and I write to you
out of a time warp the last I knew it was mid June so. Now tis
mid August and the Sun indeed sets in a very different way.
the Broken Radar Spins above the limply hanging flags.

this is the house
we live here

no smoking

← AS VIEWED FROM Bow (i.e. here)

to mean a challenge, the seamen knew that any blatant act of enmity, especially this early in a long voyage, would upset the delicate emotional balance that kept the crew in line. It was still too early to say how the chips would fall, for the word had come down that we were not going to the Mediterranean for forty-five days, as scheduled. Instead we were headed southeast, toward Angola and then around the Cape of Good Hope to Japan. This meant we were going to be on the ship for at least three months. The union contract made it clear that once you signed overseas articles you had to stay on the ship until the final port of return in the United States, or for six months. This also meant I had gotten myself into a lot more than I had bargained for. The cook gave the call that signaled the beginning of breakfast. We all silently filed up to the counter and ordered our eggs. Out of the corner of his eye, Ned glared at me. The more he thought about it, the more he hated me for getting an ordinary's job when he was stuck working in the mess. And everyone else in the crew knew exactly how he felt.

※

The SS *Rose City* was 894 feet long, 105 feet wide, and 64 feet deep. She looked unnaturally big even from a distance. She first appeared as a great metal wall that towered above the trees lining the river by the dock at Camden, New Jersey, where we boarded her. Unladen she could reach a maximum speed of 17.6 knots, plowing through the seas, her deck a good forty feet above the water. Fully laden she reached a maximum of 16.5 knots, her deck only eight or ten feet above the surface.

The house, located on the stern, was a solid square structure with flying wings jutting out on either side of the bridge.

The forward deck of the *Rose City,* from midship toward the bow

Before the house, running down the entire length of the ship
to the bow, were dozens of steel pipes, the cargo lines, some
a few inches wide, others five or six feet. In the center of the
ship they converged on either the port or starboard manifolds,
each being a great iron jam of valves that hooked into the refinery pipelines and regulated the flow of oil into or out of the
twenty-four giant tanks that lay below the iron deck.

The forepeak was an all-purpose room on the bow where
forward lines, paint, and miscellaneous tools were stowed. Just
off it was the machine shop. Above the foredeck, the two anchor blocks sat squarely before the hawse pipes, down which
ran the massive chains that held the three-ton anchors. The
view of the ship from the bow was the most inspiring: The
labyrinth of pipes that trailed back down to the house was lost
in the sheer length of the ship, a lesson in perspective.

The house, from midship toward the stern

The stern had a storeroom similar to that on the bow. It was there that the crew assembled to begin securing the deck for the two-week journey to Africa. The Chief strutted out and gave the Bosun a series of directives in his Kentucky drawl before going off to oversee the operations in the pump room. In order for the ship to sail we had to pump in thousands of gallons of seawater for ballast. The ship was little more than a floating oilcan. To be caught in a storm with the tanks empty would undoubtedly end in the ship's capsizing. But such technicalities were the officers' concern—we were busy stowing the lines.

The Bosun, as usual, manned the winch. He didn't have to work on deck if he didn't choose to. His job was officially an administrative one: organize the crew and assign them their jobs. But Dave Martin was an old fighter, trying to get over a bad stroke he had suffered a few years earlier. To work was to

The forward deck of the *Rose City,* from midship toward the bow

prove he still had it in him. And he wasn't proving it just to himself.

Three of us went down below and waited for the first line to come through the hatch. When the Bosun got the winch going, Jimmy passed it down and we laid the line in even folds along the floor of the deck. Bud curtly told me what to do, annoyed if I appeared to be putting too much effort into it.

"Let the winch do the work!"

I was slow in learning the basic tenets of modern seamanship.

The stern lines took about thirty to forty-five minutes to stow. By the time the last line dropped through the hatch, the pile of rope was nearly twelve feet square and six feet high. Once the hatch was sealed, we walked up to the bow to stow the forward lines. Despite my naïveté I began to realize the advantage a supertanker had over smaller ships. The five-minute walk from one end to the other essentially meant a five-minute work break. If several of us had to go up, we would go in shifts so that the time it took for the first man to leave and the last to arrive was generally about ten minutes. It didn't matter if the Captain was watching from the bridge; we all seemed to be following orders. Peanuts was the master at avoiding work. The first day on the ship he reprimanded me for running to fetch a wrench. "Never run on a ship! Always walk. You're not in a hurry to go anywhere," he told me.

Halfway to the bow he would often remember he had forgotten some "very important" tool, or suddenly decide he had to go to the bathroom. The latter was his favorite excuse. "Gotta go surge one," he would declare, and then he'd disappear for a good quarter of an hour, or however long he figured the job at hand would take. It was a fine art he had clearly cultivated over many years at sea.

The morning's work was relatively painless. By our ten a.m. coffee break, all of the aft and most of the forward lines had been stowed. The Bosun, as was his way, knocked us off ten minutes early so we'd have plenty of time to amble down the deck to the house.

Jake and I had climbed down from the foredeck and were beginning our walk back when he stopped and picked up a wrench.

"Always carry something," he said, acting out a potential encounter with the Chief.

Standing five-five, Jake was by far the smallest man aboard, and, clearly, after thirty-seven years at sea, he had cultivated the role of jokester. The Bosun, on the other hand, while not much taller, was infamous as a brawler. His years in the boxing rings of Philadelphia came in particularly handy, given the bars he frequented and the people he met inside them. But Jake didn't have that brute physical training to handicap his smallness. Always one to avoid a fight, Jake made his name as a clown.

CHAPTER 4

COFFEE BREAK WAS ANIMATED that morning. The ship had broken free of the river at about nine a.m. and was now sailing off the coast of Maryland. The crew sat around the lounge, the Bosun orchestrating a general mood of good cheer by telling his peculiar brand of dirty jokes and initiating a discussion about some of the other old-timers from the Philadelphia hall. I grabbed a cup and sat in a corner of the room, listening. My hands were already beginning to blister; I had neglected to bring work gloves with me, and the ship's store, the "Captain's Locker," wouldn't be open for another week.

Just as he knocked us off early for coffee, the Bosun didn't make us get back to work for a full five minutes after we were supposed to return (10:15). As we went back on deck, Billy looked around and started singing "By the sea, by the sea, by the beautiful sea." I laughed nervously but, as usual, he ignored me.

After the lines were stowed, we had to stow the gangway. Mounted on the starboard side, the gangway was less efficient than those of over three hundred years ago. A huge metal contraption, it was fastened over the side of the ship only twenty feet above the angry, churning wake. To move it to its raised berth amid the pipes was a simple task—in theory. In practice, it took hours.

Of the two huge booms that hung off the key masts at the center of the ship, only one was of any practical use in the moving of the gangway. Climbing out onto the gangway, Bud and Billy had to attach chains to its rickety frame while hanging above the water. The Bosun sat at the winch controls, ready to raise the block and tackle that had to be rigged to the chains that hung from the railings. This process in itself took more than an hour, most of the crew pulling the lines that moved the seventy-foot boom. Every time we got it moving the right way the wind would catch it, swinging the boom wildly around. At one point Jimmy desperately lashed the runner rope to the gypsy head before momentum might cause the boom to crash into the key mast and snap, destroying the countless pipes below and generating sparks that would start a chain reaction of explosions, ending in the complete destruction of the ship. After an hour my arms ached to the point where making a fist caused searing pain. The rest of the crew had to work around me. As we tugged on the ropes—a nautical reincarnation of the Iwo Jima Memorial—I was a fifth wheel, like a tedious visitor who was wholly ineffectual, yet here to stay.

Bud laughed about it. "And then there's Moynihan, pulling on ropes that don't go anywhere." The rest of the crew didn't bother to say anything.

The last sliver of land slipped out of sight about two that afternoon. We all paused for one final look at home. Billy looked away. "That's the last we'll see for a long time." The crew silently returned to work. The breeze picked up as we got farther out to sea, and the ocean became a rich dark blue. I asked the Bosun about the color, having seen only the algae-filled waters that hugged the shorelines. The Bosun stopped and looked up at me.

"How many times have you been to sea, John?" he asked me with both a smile and suspicion.

"This is my first time, Bos," I answered. When he heard that, he nodded knowingly; things were coming together as far as the Mystery of Moynihan was concerned.

The 4–8 watch was knocked off after the three-o'clock coffee break. Billy had the wheel first, so Jake and I, even though we were on watch, had to keep working until five. The special advantage of the 4–8 watch is that there is only one hour during the day (4:00 to 5:00) when you have to work without being paid overtime. Both the 8–12 and the 12–4 watches, because they are on duty between nine and five (i.e., the standard working day), lose four hours of overtime a day. We, on the other hand, could earn up to seven hours of overtime on weekdays, and fifteen on weekends (when the regular sea watch counts as OT).

Five o'clock found the crew grumpy and tired. The gangway ended up taking all afternoon to secure, the obsolete winch-and-boom system with which we had to move it being more of a hassle than a help. Just inside the hatchway that let us into the house was the laundry room where we washed up. The jar of lanolin sat above the sink from that day on as the god of hygiene, for without it we would all probably have the grime of the SS *Rose City* caked on our hands to this day.

After showering (seamen are notoriously clean; one story

that circulated among the crew concerned an SIU man who, when the ship was sinking, ran to the bathroom to wash up before getting in the lifeboat) the crew lined up for dinner. Jake ate quickly so he could relieve Billy in time for dinner. As it was still light out, there was no need for me to go on lookout, so they sent for me on the bridge for my first lesson at the wheel.

The stairwell that ran through the center of the house was a cold metallic spiral that knew only the fluorescent flickerings of the overhead lights and the *clack-clack* of heavy work boots on its linoleum steps. But sterile as it was through the first seven stories, the long flight from the last residential deck to the bridge was peculiarly foreboding. Longer than the rest, this flight was unlit, save for a dark red exit sign that burned at the top of the stairs. It took a good effort to open the heavy metal door that sealed off the stairwell, but once open, it slammed against the bulkhead with a resounding crash. This of course shattered the tense quiet of the bridge, causing officers and men alike to jump and narrow their eyes to annoyed stares.

It was always "lights-out" on the bridge, hence that final dark flight. The red and green glow cast from the electrical equipment was interrupted only by the sharp white triangle of light that beat down on the sea charts. It was not a large space; on watch it took only seven long strides to traverse before I had to pivot and pace back to the other wall. Dividing the bridge in half was a rigid metal containing wall that left only three or four feet on either side to get around. Before it stood the radar, the compass, and the other electrical navigational devices that never worked but impressed stockholders and Coast Guard inspectors. The wheel was mounted on a long gray metal console. My devotion to Errol Flynn had long given me a quixotic vision of the man at the wheel. There Jake stood, the able-bodied seaman from North Philadelphia, fearlessly guiding the SS *Rose City* through the dark, restless seas of the North Atlantic. The responsibility and power had in no way diminished since the day Captain Blood had leaped from the yardarm and, wrestling the great wooden wheel out of its spinning fury with all the might his two strong arms could muster, guided the ship through the battle. But these days the wheel itself had shrunk to a foot in diameter, a metal and plastic tool that was thrown on automatic pilot ninety percent of the time. It was the other ten percent that counted.

Jake greeted me warmly. He had come to see in me the same youthful anticipation and excitement that he knew when he first shipped out, forty years earlier. He took me under his wing, was determined to teach me the skills and art of the sea, lest I be victimized by my simple lack of experience. Set in the center of the console, the wheel was surrounded on either side by the outside lighting controls, the PA system, and a number of salt-covered knobs and dials that had long since rusted fast. The wheel was situated at waist height, allowing for a relaxed stance, both hands resting on it without being too high or too low. Pointing to the circular gauge just above it, Jake began his first lesson on how to man the wheel.

"This here's the automatic pilot. Right now it's set at one hundred twenty degrees, putting us on a course due southeast. Now, you turn it off by hitting this button here, and you're on manual control. To steer the ship you've gotta compensate for the lee and the tides. It's usually okay if you stay within a few degrees, but no more." He stole a glance back at the Chief, who was behind the partition, hunched over the charts, plotting our course. "If she starts right, turn the wheel a few degrees to the left and it'll bring her back on. Right now she's pulling right, so you've gotta keep your eye on the gauge. Now, right there's the overhead compass. Neither one of 'em is totally on the mark, so I keep somewhere in between the two."

He called out to the Chief. "Mate, is it okay if the kid takes the wheel now?"

The Chief lumbered over to the console and rocked his thickset body on his heels, contemplating the question. The sun had set but the gray twilight skies gave us a fair visibility. The Chief stared out the window and quietly said it was all right, then returned to his duties behind the partition. Jake stepped aside and let me take over the wheel. From up on the bridge I could see the whole expanse of the ship plunging through the water. With the wheel in my hands I felt the ship come alive; it was no longer a shaky float in a large body of water.

The first sensation was the immediate contact with the shudders and tremors of the ship. Between the grinding vibrations of the all-powerful engine room and the pounding of the sea at her unyielding steel sides, the ship was an animate mover. She pushed her way through the ocean, raising her bow with every swell and hurtling back down with a deafening crescendo. I could feel the movement, the huge screw in the back working to propel her forward. The horizon became less of a definition between sea and sky than a tangible object that could be sought, reached, left behind.

Then again, being on the wheel was rarely a metaphysical experience: Within seconds of my taking over, the ship was swaying right. I hesitantly pulled the wheel left, but without result. Five degrees, six degrees, seven degrees. The ship finally responded at ten, coming slowly off her right course and swinging left. The problem was that although I had returned the wheel to 120, the ship continued to swing, rolling way to the left. Jake, while not saying very much, kindly pointed this out in a voice low enough to escape the Chief's ears. Then again, he didn't want to be held responsible for a mid-Atlantic course change, either. I made up for the leftward pull by steering five degrees right, and then, as the ship responded, brought the wheel around to three degrees left. The first crisis was over.

I held the wheel that first evening for the better part of an hour. Jake stood by, telling stories of past ships' crews and their follies, and I began to get a feel for the mechanics of quartermastering. He was a cantankerous sort. His stories were punctuated with wild expressions or laughs of disbelief, as his subjects were always some outrageous character or circumstance. In his sharp tenor, he entertained me, shortening the long watch with a few anecdotes. Though he had to keep his voice down to a low murmur so as not to disturb the Chief, he

WAVES

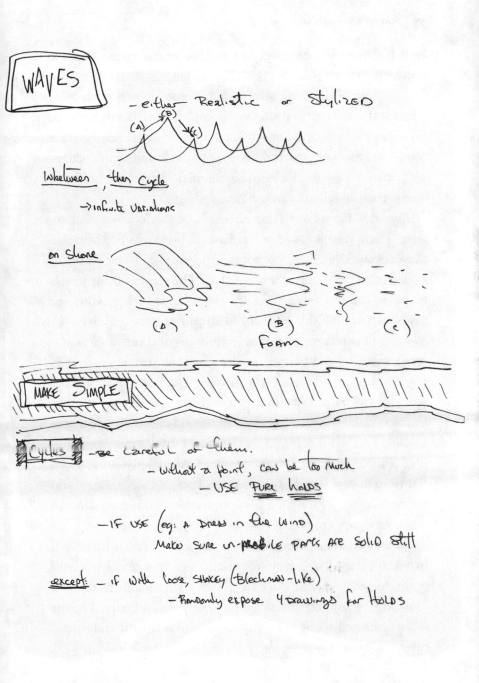

— either Realistic   or   Stylized

(A) (B) (C)

<u>Inbetween</u>, then Cycle

→ Infinite Variations

<u>on Shore</u>

(A)   (B)   (c)

foam

MAKE SIMPLE

Cycles — Be Careful of them.
— Without a point, can be too much
— USE PURE <u>holds</u>

— IF USE (eg: A DRESS in the wind)
Make sure un-profile parts are solid still

<u>except</u>: — if with loose, shakey (Blechman-like)
— Randomly expose 4 drawings for Holds

kept his monologue going, avoiding as much as possible the monotony of silence.

There was little time after watch before I had to turn in. The spectre of the 12–4 watch waking me at 3:20 a.m., a mere seven and a half hours away, kept my nocturnal activity to a few beers, the better part of a movie in the lounge, and a chapter or two of a book. With uncharacteristic discipline, I bunked out at ten and fell into an exhausted sleep.

Rap, rap. Lights on. Time check. Lookout local weather report. There was no avoiding it: Even if I went to bed at eight, they always woke me too soon. And unlike life at home, I pulled myself out of bed immediately. The tension from always being on call was fast exceeding tolerable levels. My cabin was my sanctuary. Within it I could dream of home and N. C. Wyeth's illustrations of pirates, while beyond my door was a very unsettling reality. This was my first full day at sea. Yesterday had begun with land still in view. Then, if worse came to worst, I could always swim to shore. Now I was trapped by the limitless miles of ocean between my world and theirs. Just outside my room lay a crew of suspicious seamen who, while not preoccupied with me, regarded me as an antiquarian might a Babylonian curiosity. Beyond my door was Billy Mahoney, and he was a fight looking for a place to happen. As it turned out, I was a very happening place.

I was still unqualified to work the wheel, and with it still being too dark for anyone to teach me any more, I inadvertently forced Jake and Billy to split my wheel shift again. On lookout you could strike a comfortable pose and relax. On the wheel you had to be on your toes; even with the automatic pilot, the mate was right there issuing commands.

I drank my coffee in the lounge and then, trying to appear confident, made my way up the stairwell and through the bridge to the port wing for lookout. Bud looked up from his trance and collected himself.

"There's a ship over on the starboard side. Other than that there's nothing," he told me.

He said nothing more, gladly leaving me on the wing. The night was untouched even by the first hint of day, and a strong warm wind buffeted the bridge. I pushed my hair out of my eyes and wrapped myself in my jacket. Leaning against the rail, I looked out into the dark. The stars were amazing, great illuminations that covered the entire expanse of the sky with unexpected brilliance. We had definitely left civilization behind. One look at the scowl on Billy's face as he paced back and forth in the wheelhouse like a caged wolf could tell you that.

Somewhere in the back of my mind I recalled a half-forgotten scene from the film version of *The Glass Menagerie*. In it the son stands on the bridge of some forlorn freighter during the midnight watch. "That was the time, the ghost watch," I thought I heard him say, "when no one else on the ship is up, and you sink back into your memories, and why you came out here." I'd not read nor seen the play in years, and I didn't even know the exact words. But I knew exactly what he meant. There on the port wing I recalled the sentiment.

CHAPTER 5

AT SEA: THIRD DAY OUT

Well, I guess you could say the proverbial shit hit the fan today. Now it's around that I'm DPM's progeny. Jake, who has been showing me the ropes, and Billy are now alienated. More on this as it develops.

—SEA LOG 6/14/80

The most satisfying aspect of life on the ship was the constant supply of food. Unlike the university, the ship provided three square meals a day, and plenty in between. Miguel, the cook, soon became the leading figure on A deck, perpetually running back and forth between the lounge and the mess, talking to himself. "Jesus Christ motherfucker goddamn! What the fuck! Ho-ho, hee-hee . . ." And so he would rattle on.

In the morning, when the tired crew would line up for breakfast, Miguel's good humor was blunted only by the growlings of the steward. The old black man, no matter how loud you yelled out your order, could never hear you. Thus each meal became a constant series of shouting matches between him and crew.

But though the *Rose City* was hailed by the crew as one of the best feeders on the seas, whatever pleasures there were to be had at mealtime were dampened by the tension in the mess.

First there were the officers, who joined us in the meal line but ate in their private mess at tables laid out by Pete and Ned. They moved with authority, their very bearing emanating a powerful sense of command. Chests out, backs arched, chins down, they bore a military air lent them by their drill training at the various officers' academies they had attended, and thereby also had the soldier's gift for intimidation.

Standing in line, I tried not to give away my nervousness. I'd silently grab my tray and silverware and, sandwiched between officers and men, would wait for my food. During the first week of the voyage everybody was antsy. A new crew, a long voyage, and an uncertainty as to what the wife would be up to during the months of absence put the whole crew on edge. In the crew mess, Billy and the boys covered up their displeasure at being away with loud talk and pointed exclamations. The old-timers began what was to become a predictable cycle of reminiscence. I took to sitting at their table to hear the fascinating oral histories of their time-lost world. My imagined visions of the Merchant Marine, it became clear, were not idle fantasies at all, but rather an inherited memory. There was, in fact, a time when one could crew on an old freighter and sail to Singapore, when the dollar was king and an American on the town could have more women, wine, and wangdoodle than he could possibly hope to handle. Another reason I sat with the old-timers was because they were just that. Age had mellowed even Dave Martin, who once claimed, while on shore leave for fifteen days in San Francisco, to have gotten into nineteen fights. My ignorance and weakness were not as important to them as was my youth, on which they looked with nostalgia. Sitting with the old-timers also meant I could keep my back to the boys' table and eat my meals with the least amount of hassle.

Our first weekend at sea ended with stocking the lifeboats. The Chief stopped calling all hands; now only those on watch or who wished to earn overtime showed up for work during the day. There were only two lifeboats, one on either side of the house. Twenty-foot red metal craft, they were stuffed with as many survival supplies as possible. In the cabinets under the seats, cans of fresh water and food, smeared with axle grease to prevent rusting, were jammed in. Other storage spaces contained radios, flares, rope, spears, extra oars, and, of course, a powerful outboard and a supply of gas.

The physical labor was good therapy as far as I was concerned. Forming a chain, we passed the supplies up out of the storeroom and into the boats all day long. The Atlantic was smooth and the sky sharply clear. I was beginning to feel more relaxed with the circumstances of nautical maintenance. Then Ned approached me on the stern.

He had obviously come down from the kitchen for a particular reason; lunch was almost ready, and he had much to do before an entire hungry crew showed up on A deck. He stopped me from whatever I was trying to do simply by his curious and threatening countenance.

"Hey, man, how'd you get the ordinary's job?" There was almost a complaining whine in his angry Philadelphia drawl.

"Uh, in New York." My response was far from satisfactory,

and I knew it. My eyes all too often betray otherwise hidden guilt.

"Well"—he paused, wondering how to pursue and confirm his conviction that I had usurped his job—"when did it go up? What time?"

I said something about morning in as matter-a-fact a voice as I could conjure.

"Morning, huh?" was his reply. He frowned and shrugged, stuffing his hands into his pockets and turning away in disgust. At least he'd not gotten anything out of me, I thought to myself. But the confrontation established Ned as my first open enemy on the ship. When lunch hour came around I closed myself in my cabin and wrote a long passage in my journal. Things were potentially very ugly.

At 1:10 the watchman came by to see if I wanted afternoon overtime. I put on my work boots and trudged down the stairwell to get my orders from the Bosun. The next day we were to begin Butterworth operations. Apparently that involved cleaning the tanks somehow, but I really had no idea when, what, or where. But for now we were instructed to continue scouring the ship and cleaning up.

There is always that breathtaking moment when one who hasn't seen the ocean for months comes over the last hill and first catches sight of the sea stretching out from the beach to the horizon. Used to the interruptions of hills and houses, the city dweller involuntarily stops in awe. The sheer geometry of that cutoff point between an irregular surface and a perfect sphere is at once startling and humbling.

Out at sea this sensation is doubled. Not only does one see the limitless ocean before him, but behind him also. No amount of rationalization—the comforting thoughts that man's nautical inventiveness can secure safe passage across the waters—will calm the frightening vulnerability that seizes you when you look around and realize that there is nothing for 360 degrees. As strong and steely as the supertanker SS *Rose City* may have been, it would have been a simple matter for the ocean to twist her into a pretzel and drag her down into the dark folds of the deep.

The view from the stern was the most impressive. The huge screw that moved the ship discharged a great explosion of white water that ceaselessly frothed and writhed in our immediate wake and then smoothed itself out. It was as if some great carpenter took a plane to a wooden sea, the wood chips furiously flying at contact, the rough board becoming glasslike with each stroke of his hand. Alas, for this carpenter, the wood tended to diffuse, and within minutes the calm path of water that we carved was erased by the bucking of the tides. Nonetheless, from the stern you could see the earth's perfect sphere plotted out with a great white line that radiated from the ship to a point beyond the horizon.

Bud, Jimmy, and I leaned against the rail during a lull in the afternoon's work and quietly watched the ocean. The two of them knew each other well enough from the hall to be relaxed in each other's company. We idled, and our small talk gradually picked up into a full-fledged conversation. Bud squinted in the hot sun and looked down at me.

"Are you related to the famous Moynihan?"

"Yeah," was my reply. *Shit!* was my thought, but having told the Old Man one story, I couldn't change it now.

"How so?"

"He's my father."

Bud started laughing, almost nervously. "No shit! I didn't think there was any fucking way. I just took a wild guess."

Jimmy, who was looking on, grunted with interest; he was likewise impressed. "He's a good man," he said, nodding his head up and down.

Bud mimicked his movements, but the conversation was over. We stood around in silence for a few minutes.

It had become too awkward to even bother trying to cover up the new order of things with pointless talk. I made some excuse for myself and walked back to the house. As I disappeared I didn't even worry about whether the two of them would start talking behind my back; what's the point in yelling at the given? There was a bathroom between the back of the house and the stack deck that was rarely used. I closed myself in there and locked the door. The only thing more frightening than realizing the dangers of the ocean when you're out in the middle of it is realizing that the ship you're on isn't any safer.

After Bud and Jimmy found out my true identity I spent the remainder of the day quietly performing my duties. Jake gave me another lesson at the wheel and told me a few more stories of his first trip. He was becoming increasingly eager to put me on the right track, so far as sailing was concerned. The wheel, likewise, softened its temper. After the night's watch, the Chief, sauntering over to the console, looked up from his clipboard and nodded permission for me to work the wheel. I still wasn't going to be allowed to steer in narrow sea channels, but at least the heat was off from Jake and Billy. With one simple nod the Chief had created equity in the work on the 4–8 watch. I was an established ordinary. I may not have known what I was doing on the wheel, but that was far from the point. The point was, I didn't have to burden Jake and Billy with splitting my wheel watch. I allowed myself a wry smile. What would the executives of Texaco do if they knew a twenty-year-old beer-drinking ex-hippie who had been out to sea for only two and a half days was controlling the destiny of one of their largest supertankers?

It soon became clear that other than work and sleep there was very little that successfully distracted me from ruminating on the long months to come. While the lounge never wanted for conversation, the crew rarely if ever spoke to one another beyond an exchange of casual anecdotes. This was partly the way of the sea: You don't stick your nose in some-one else's business; the further you probe, the more trouble you're looking for. Occasion-ally at coffee, or at a quiet moment in a drunk, someone might volunteer a tale of his past that wasn't the standard comic rap. But at this early stage in the voyage no one wanted to think about his own wife, let alone listen to some-one else's troubles.

Reading was one alternative to the blanket homesickness

that had settled on the crew. Locked away in my cabin I could attempt to restore my lost peace of mind with vestiges of my intellectual past, but I soon realized that the noble stack of classics I had brought with me were doomed to fall before *John Carter of Mars* and the Gormenghast trilogy.

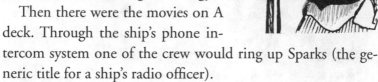

Then there were the movies on A deck. Through the ship's phone intercom system one of the crew would ring up Sparks (the generic title for a ship's radio officer).

"Sparks, how about a movie?"

After a few minutes the TV would crackle to life in the darkened lounge. It seemed that Sparks had a Betamax hidden away amid his electronic labyrinth, and, like some omnipotent sorcerer, he wielded the power of diversion or tedium over the melancholy crew of the *Rose City*. There was an unlikely assortment of films, however; Woody Allen and F. Scott Fitzgerald films are not especially popular among seamen. Fortunately he had a tape of *High Plains Drifter*.

There was, as it turned out, another source of films on board: The Captain's Locker, the ship's store, where gloves, cigarettes, and other assorted necessities were sold by the officers to the crew, sponsored a ship's library of reel-films and a projector. A screen in the officers' mess provided the backdrop for such hits as *The Great Santini, Boxcar Bertha,* and *Eye of the Tiger*. The featured attraction was the ship's one and only porno movie, shown first forward, and then in reverse. After a while it became difficult to tell the difference.

Down in the lounge Billy, Ned, and Charlie, the QMED, were in command. I drifted down with a beer and slunk into a chair to see what was up. They had broken out coffee cans and buckets to serve as coolers for their beer. Unlike myself, desperately trying to abstain from drink and smoke for a few months, they were ready to tear it up. Before long it was decided that a movie in the officers' mess was in order.

The officers' mess was really no different from ours, except for the movie screen and the personal service they were given by the Steward's Department. Billy dragged the projector into the room and we all settled down with our beer for the movie. Miguel joined us before long—it made no difference to him that he had seen all the movies on the ship fifty times; he went for the ritual. Billy and Ned were drinking gin and tonics from a pitcher, and it became clear as the movie progressed that they were becoming a team.

There is a special art to watching movies at sea. With every action on the screen there must be a string of commentaries and expletives. Bud was the master of the play-by-play; his running analysis of the film's progress kept everyone in stitches, and the story in perspective. Billy and Ned were pretty good at the game, but to them the importance lay in the party that went along with watching a flick. Back and forth, they poured each other drinks, aping the old-timers in their heyday. The more they drank, the stronger they felt. The stronger (and drunker) they felt, the less they regretted being at sea.

At one point the film jammed and the revelry was broken. Billy, who had taken up position by the projector in order to run the show, had trouble getting it back in sync. I made my way over to where he was fiddling in an attempt to apply my cinematic expertise.

Billy glowered at me. "That's all right, college boy, I can fix it."

CHAPTER 6

THAT NIGHT I HAD A VIVID DREAM. I was back at the university and haunted by all those things that never quite got done, all those half-fulfilled commitments and plans. Somewhere in the dream landscape: "I can remember scattered fragments . . ." is how my journal reads in the dream. I stand before a typical dorm, staring at it from the other side of a hurricane fence. Unlike in most dreams, there is a vital immediacy to the situation. As I emerge from the woods and make my way to the dorm I am overwhelmed by the sense of failure that has haunted me since I left school. Even in my dreams I am not free of regret.

Inside the dorm there is the expected collection of familiar and important friends. (Each one has affected me somehow, and now they chase me out to sea.) Before them is a series of magical candles, each tall and thin, save for a great black one that has been fitted into a human head. A particularly macabre friend of mine appears only to play a satanic record, filling the room with evil chantings. The candles are lit, and the room is overwhelmed with their dark burnings. I am then forced to

lost Faerie tales - Fragments of Twilight

AS LOVECRAFT IS TO POE, L.F.T. IS TO Borges

Black Cathedral of Brasov

Bloodfog
long black veil
Scare Crow + Jack o'lantern
Pagan IDOL
Purple SKY
"THE STARE"
WOODPile /Figure in white
Turtles + Dragon
OLD lady + the TOAD
Catacombs
Stealing in the Mirror
Artist/Iron Penohorg Battle of will Power — Sex Murder

Warrior/Pond/Demigod
Warrior + sword (looks up)
Owl Nailed to tree/Barn
Winter Cat
Sirens + Banshees
People of the Forest (Pulliam milkout)

Blind sailor/Woar
witch + kids/boiling pot
Ghoul in Attic
SPHYNX in Forest
"little People"

recite a demonic enchantment. That is when I first hear the Voices.

They come from some undefined dimension. It is not a question of heaven or hell, up or down. They come from beyond, and they are not of my subconscious. They simply are. And it terrifies me. Later I will read in my journal cryptic statements heard in the dream: "That's it! Can't you see? That's what it is! The chance/simultaneous happenings are the key . . ." But now the Voices dominate my thoughts. They cry out that they are not evil, but I am far too shaken to listen to them.

"They never want me to get there."

Then I woke up.

Then I *really* woke up as I heard the watch awaken the other two on my watch. . . .

Thus I concluded the fevered account of the dream in my journal. It was the first dream I had on the ship, and it left me feeling haunted and uneasy. It would be another two hemispheres, twenty-three time zones, and three and a half months before I heard the Voices again.

Butterworth operations (tank cleaning) involve hours of backbreaking preparation work, and hours of absolute inactivity when finally under way. After a tanker dispatches its load at the refinery, its tanks must be cleaned before a new load can be picked up. The first step is flushing out the twenty-four great tanks with ocean water. Six stories down, in the pump room, the third mate took Billy and me to open the sea pumps and send thousands of gallons of water rushing through the ship's massive pump network. Like everything else on the ship, the sea valves were constructed for the least possible efficiency. It took us fifteen minutes just to open the first valve, straining on the great rusted wheel while the mate stood over us, watching. Once it was open, the rumbling of the water resonated throughout the ship.

It is not difficult to tell whether a tanker is cleaning its tanks. Having washed, buffeted, and generally rinsed out the tanks, we could see the dirty water discharged from the side of the ship through the manifold. For hundreds of miles we left an oily slick on the surface of the ocean without thinking twice about it. Anywhere in the Atlantic, Indian, or Pacific Oceans the residue of tankers can be seen. At one point we followed the course of another tanker that had left a trail of pollution across several latitudes.

The Butterworth machines were stored up in the forepeak. They were little more than mobile garden hoses: seventy-foot lengths of thick rubber tubes mounted on five-foot-high wheels that we rolled out onto the main deck. Attached to the end of each of the half dozen hoses was a twenty-pound metal contraption that looked like a heavy duty sprinkler. It was through the sheer force of its spraying power that the 216,000 square feet of each tank were to be cleaned.

The day was clear and breezy as we began our work. The Bosun had called all hands, and up on the deck the tired crew shuffled to the forepeak. Jake, in a better mood than usual, went into an animated demonstration of rope work. With a supple flip of his wrist he conjured a series of intricate and powerful knots. The others sat back and watched with distracted amusement; attention was given to anything that passed the time during work.

The Bosun arrived on the bow and assigned us to various chores while he kept the Chief busy with the logistics of the operation. It was a good hour or so before all the machines were rolled out to their working positions. Not only did each machine weigh several hundred pounds, but the countless pipes that crisscrossed the deck compounded the difficulty of the task.

Except for a hatch leading to a staircase, the only openings to the tanks were the small, round apertures through which the Butterworth hoses were lowered. Using a T-wrench, Bud and Billy went down both sides of the deck unbolting and removing the heavy iron covers. It was then up to the rest of us to move the machines over to the open hatches and, screwing the nozzles onto the hoses, make ready to begin spraying. The work on the starboard side was not all that difficult, as there were only a few pipes that got in the way. But to gain access to the port deck we had to roll the machines up a ramp and over the great lengths of the steam pipes that stood three feet off the ground and ran all the way down to the house. Some of the crew suggested we roll the bloody things all the way back to the stern and around the other side of the house instead. There was, after all, the attraction of being able to waste a good twenty to thirty minutes on the job that way. But the Bosun would hear nothing of it.

The hoses themselves were raised and lowered by water pressure, the other end of the hose being locked into one of the central pipes. At the Chief's command the pump would be thrown on and thousands of gallons of water would rush through the lowered hoses and set their sprinklers in motion. It was a sight reminiscent of the Yellowstone geysers. At regular four-minute intervals the open hatches would erupt in a scalding shower of water, sending the crew running for cover. At the first level (the hoses were lowered to the bottom of the tank, about sixty feet, and systematically raised ten feet every forty minutes) the shower was not much more than an occasional three-foot burst, but at the highest level the fusillade of hot water made the area of the deck around the machines unapproachable.

Once a routine had been established I became sure of what my job was. My complete lack of experience and knowledge of the technical jargon made me something of a liability in particularly difficult operations. As a rule I simply shut up and watched, trying to catch on before my ignorance caught up to me. It was the small things, like the Bosun's having to explain to me the difference between a hatchet and a crescent wrench, that annoyed the younger crew. The old-timers were pretty much disgusted with everything anyway, so my ignorance was only one of a shipful of gripes.

At the end of the morning's work the ship was suddenly overtaken by a rain squall, and the crew took refuge in the forepeak. Billy, Jake, Bud, and I stood in the hatchway, watching the waves of cold rain sweep across the water and over the ship. It was a welcome break from work, and one that we were being paid for.

There was, as usual, little or no conversation apart from complaints about the job or the officers. Then Bud let go some comment about my father and the forepeak was suddenly filled with a dead silence.

Billy and Jake, when they finally got it straight that, yes, my father was in fact a senator, were speechless for a moment. I silently nodded that it was true and turned away from the look of shock in their eyes and hurt on their faces.

Joe was the first to react. No less awed than the other two, he was also very impressed. Meeting someone so close to the top, so near the power source, frightened him a little, and his composure mellowed.

"Monahan, eh? He's a good man." I had caught him off guard: not a dumb-ass college scab, but a personification of the American class system.

Billy and Jake, once over the initial shock, suddenly grew totally alienated. Billy's face quickly darkened and became ugly.

"Your father's a fucking senator? What the fuck are you doing out here?" he screamed at me.

Jake stared at me for a moment and then looked away and began muttering to the other collected crew members. He had taken to calling me his protégé, proud of the skills he had been teaching me. Now I had betrayed him, and he was unforgiving.

Billy kept screaming at me: "What is it, senator's son? Can't your daddy find you a job in Washington?" Then it hit him why I got the job as opposed to Ned, who had waited in the union hall for three months, and he walked away in disgust. The rain had ended, but it was lunchtime, or close enough to it that the rest of the crew followed Billy back to the house. On the long walk back I spoke to no one, and no one spoke to me. Once again that sick feeling of adolescent anxiety reasserted itself. I was on my own until our return to America, more than three months from now. I filed into the washroom and, standing in the far corner, waited for the rest of the silent crew to finish at the sink. At lunch that afternoon Ned did not look up at me once while serving the stew. The word was out.

The day after I was exposed I didn't work any overtime. Holing up in my room, I attempted to escape the hostile stares on A deck. The cabin faced the stern, and as such let in no light. The principal dominating feature of the house was the chimney stack that shot up to a height some 120 feet above the main deck. Surrounding it was the stack deck, which connected to B deck via a small bridge that spanned the gap between the house and the stack proper. It was the alternative lounge where the crew drank, set up lawn chairs, and sunned themselves. The end result was that any cabin that faced the stern had but a single view—the stack. Its shadow made for perpetual twilight.

All day I lay on my bunk, reading *Dispatches*. The immediacy of the writing overwhelmed me and I began to have serious fantasies of riding into battle with Errol Flynn's son, Sean, on my Harley-Davidson 900, and grabbing the next chopper to Saigon.

When Joe called me for the afternoon watch, I stayed in the lounge until five, thinking that since I wasn't working overtime I wasn't needed until my turn at the wheel. When the Bosun came up to see where I was, I caught an earful.

"What the hell are you doing? You're supposed to be down there with the rest of the guys!" He wasn't mad, particularly; he knew I wasn't aware of all the rules, but he didn't at any cost want the Chief to find out someone had missed mandatory work. I wasn't free to sit in the lounge until five. It was the way the company got its money's worth: Only on the weekends were the men on watch not responsible for some sort of manual labor when they weren't on lookout or at the wheel.

I ran out on deck and met up with the rest of the crew in the forepeak. Billy was the first to yell at me.

"What the fuck is this, senator's son? Whatta you been doing, jerking off in your room?" and so on. I stood there dumbly and looked for something to do, but it was almost dinnertime and everyone was wrapping up. Billy didn't let up for an instant. When he wasn't razzing me, he was grimly going about his business in a raging silence. I had no choice but to take it.

Meanwhile, the sun was setting before us. The days were growing noticeably shorter; the equator was fast approaching.

The big event the first week out at sea was the pay raise. As of June sixteenth the overtime rate went up a good five percent. But though it was a breakthrough for the union, the increase did not bear close inspection. In addition to the minimum wage I was getting for standing watch, as an ordinary I would receive $4.86 an hour for weekly overtime. In other words, I wasn't even making time and a half. Weekend overtime (which included the regular watch) was a little better: I was paid $7.67 an hour, but this still meant I had to work fourteen hours a day, seven days a week, to make more than the $876.77 monthly rate.

For the old-timers the union was a favorite topic of debate. There was not a union official alive they didn't accuse of some heinous crime or other. The beefs were, however, generally not without good reason. To make pension, the brothers of the SIU had to put in twenty years. Twenty years *sea time*. Thus it took an average of forty to forty-five years for a seaman to make pension. Peanuts, Dave Martin, Jake, Joe, and their comrades back in Philadelphia had all joined up before World War II and were only now becoming eligible for retirement. The years at sea had, on the one hand, been a relief from Depression-era America, and a way to make money and have a hell of a time doing it. On the other hand, it had become the only trade and way of life they knew. The good-time Charlies of the '40s and '50s were now stuck in a dead-end job with no alternative but to follow the union bosses.

This was the main gripe the crew had with me. I was continually asked, "What the hell are you doing out here? Go back to college and make yourself a decent living." They couldn't see how someone who didn't have to be a grease monkey all his life would leave college to become just that. At the time I didn't dwell on the metaphysical nature of the question but concerned myself with not getting beaten by resentful and angry Merchant Marines.

I had no choice but to work the best I could with the crew, so the next day I returned to overtime work. The Butterworth operations (named Butterworth for the man who invented the rotating high-powered nozzle) continued in their monotonous way. Every day for the next two weeks there was no change in the routine. Stand watch, eat breakfast, work overtime tending the machines, eat lunch, work more overtime, eat dinner, stand evening watch, and catch grief from Billy the entire day. At times it was a simple gesture, like flipping the finger at me through the window when I was on the wheel and he was on lookout. Other times it was a lecture in the lounge for all to hear.

"You know what your problem is, Monahan? You've been fed on the silver spoon all your life. You're a fucking prima donna. Why don't you go back home where you belong?"

One time he was strutting around the lounge during a coffee break, yelling at me, when someone told him to "lay off the kid."

He turned and looked at me with his caustic smile, and then, walking away, said, "I don't give you too much of a hard time, do I, John?"

I muttered something about him "fucking with me all the time." He spun around and looked at me fiercely.

"You wanna fuck with me? I'll string you up from here to the key post!" He got more violent as he went on. I shrank into my seat. So much for nipping it in the bud.

On the fifth day of Butterworthing, the Chief had us begin as early as the light permitted. This didn't trouble the 4–8 watch particularly, as dawn that day was at 6:30 a.m. and we'd be making extra money on watch. As Jake put it, "If you pick up an oily rag, mark it down as 'Cleaning Oil Spill.'"

After breakfast the rest of the crew joined the three of us on deck to begin the day's work. The Bosun sent me off to get an Allen wrench, and when I returned the crew was standing around, talking in hushed and subdued tones.

Billy, looking down the hatchway to the seventh starboard tank, said, "My mother didn't raise no hero."

The others muttered their agreement and looked up uncertainly at the approaching Bosun. Being sixty pounds overweight and barely five-five, he took at least twice as long to walk the length of the deck as anyone else on board. When he finally waddled up to the hatchway he had to pause a minute

before speaking in order to catch his breath and wipe away the rivers of sweat that ran down his red swollen face.

"He really hasn't been the same since he had that stroke," one of the old-timers grumbled behind me.

The Bosun looked around and began relaying the day's orders. The crew, however, remained curiously hesitant to act upon them. Just then, Charlie, the QMED, showed up with a full complement of welding equipment. The word from the Old Man was that a crack in the superstructure between tanks seven and eight was to be repaired before we reached Cabinda, on the west coast of Africa.

There was no more putting it off, and the Bosun was now forced to ask for a volunteer to go down in the tank opposite the welder and stand ready with a fire extinguisher. The crew refused. Billy and Charlie, having joined the union at the same time and being roughly the same age, had already established themselves as buddies. But now Billy was decidedly displeased with Charlie for agreeing to be the welder. As the Bosun stood there dumbly, Joe and Jake explained the situation to me more clearly. This was strictly a voluntary job, unlike most jobs the ABs were obliged by Maritime Law to perform. (Ordinaries, being by definition unqualified, were already exempt from many of the most hazardous jobs.) However, one would make triple time for going down there, and receive three standard hours' wages in addition as a clothing allowance.

So far as I was concerned that was enough of an enticement, and I told the Bosun I'd do it. The others almost sighed with relief that the issue was settled, and that they were free of the burden. The Bosun couldn't think of an objection and gave me the go-ahead.

Now established as the point man, I was outfitted and instructed by the crew. Charlie disappeared down into the adjacent tank and his gear was lowered to him on a long, stout rope. Over by tank seven, the fire extinguisher was likewise secured and made ready to go.

"All you have to do is stand by the spot where they're coming through and make sure no fire starts up," the Bosun explained. "You know how to use one of these extinguishers?" I nodded. The Bosun, though sincere and having the best of intentions, was the master of explaining the obvious.

Everything prepared, the Chief out on deck, and Charlie in position, I climbed down into the tank. Much like a standard fire escape, the stairs that led down to the floor of the tank zigzagged six stories alongside the massive steel bulkhead.

The tank was huge, like three regulation basketball courts stacked up. Except for the entrance at the top of the stairs, the only light in the great holding vat streamed in through the hatches for the Butterworth machines. The broad beams of sunlight cut through the still steamy air and bounced off a surprisingly clean floor. It seems Mr. Butterworth knew what he was doing; the tank was completely clean of oil except for a quarter inch of residue that clung to the metal walls and floor.

I shouted up to the Bosun and the others that I was all set and they lowered the fire extinguisher down to me. I positioned myself at the crack and, pulling out the pin, made ready with the fire extinguisher.

The morning wore on, and I soon discarded my vigilant stance for a relaxed pose across from the crack. The fire extinguisher was still within easy reach; however, I no longer thought of heroically saving the ship. It dawned on me, as I sat on one of the three-foot-high pipes that ran through the tank, that not only was I making excellent money, but I was also being paid for doing virtually nothing. I was catching on to the seaman's ways.

At coffee time I was called out of the tank and joined Charlie and the first engineer, who had been supervising the welding. On the walk back to the house they debriefed me on the progress as seen from my side. The First was a grim silent man in his late fifties. Apart from our waiting in line for food together, the deck gang had little or no contact with any of the engineers. The First was a classic example of the distinctions between officers and men, and the deck and engine departments. He scowled haughtily at one and all and never uttered a word. The only time he was known to have spoken outside the engine room was to order breakfast. Not that any of the crew really cared.

Charlie and I, along with the others on deck, collected in the lounge for coffee. Charlie was his usual animated self. As the 4–8 QMED, he was better known by Billy, Jake, and me than the rest of the engine crew, since he took his breaks in the lounge with us while the rest of the ship slept. Short and muscular, he had terrible skin augmented by elaborate four-color tattoos emblazoned all over his body. On one leg was a Mayan priest dancing in full regalia. On his arm a great bird of prey searched the skies for some undefined foe. And so on. Charlie was more up in body and spirit than the rest of the crew; he intended to stay on for a year in order to make enough money to buy himself a house and some property. To him a long voyage in the Orient was a blast.

The crew didn't like the welding, so that morning they weren't concerned with Charlie's plans; they were more than a little angry with him for offering to weld the crack. I hadn't realized it, but when a tanker is light, the danger of igniting volatile fumes is at its greatest. Our captain, it suddenly occurred to me, was not only violating Coast Guard law by welding on deck, he was sending us down into vapor-filled tanks with an open flame. It also came out that the radar on the bridge had gone out the first full day at sea, and instead of stopping off in South Africa to have it repaired we were going to wait until we got to Japan. It didn't matter that we'd be going through the Straits of Malacca in typhoon season: Business is business, and the insurance will pay off anything that might go wrong. For Billy this was too much. He didn't say more than the usual bitter innuendoes at coffee, but inside him it was building up.

✳

The welding in the tank went on for two and a half days. As each session began, the descent ritual was repeated and the heightened tension returned. The dark isolation inside was blissful relief from the manic arena of the lounge. The silhouetted figures of Billy and the crew were pleasantly distant, and they were looking out for me rather than razzing me.

But the threat of disaster quickly manifested itself. The afternoon of the second day, the sounds of the welding grew noticeably louder. I looked up from my reverie to find great molten sparks shooting out of the crack and dancing across the oil-soaked floor. The Chief looked down impassively through the haze of smoke and vapor that hung trapped in the air between the hull and the deck.

The atmosphere in the lounge did not improve following this. At afternoon coffee the Bosun, leading the usual round-table discussion of the day's work, questioned me on the progress of the welding. When I told him what had gone down, the gathered crew shuddered involuntarily. Billy jumped up and went into a heated, impassioned tirade.

"Those no good motherfuckers! They don't give a shit about what happens to us! They send some kid down there who doesn't know better, and expect him to keep the ship from blowing the fuck up with a fire extinguisher?" He went on for a minute or so, pacing back and forth among the men, pausing only to gesture or suck on his cigarette.

The others sat quietly, agreeing with him but afraid of his violent temperament. Charlie squirmed in his seat and made limited attempts to defend himself. Ultimately he didn't have to. The officers wanted the job done, and he was willing to do it. It was too early in the trip for union pressure to keep him from working. In short, he didn't really give a damn if the crew didn't like his volunteering to weld; they couldn't do anything to stop him.

The old-timers started talking about other ships that had gone down under similar circumstances. Peanuts went into one particularly vivid account of an Indian ship he'd seen catch fire in San Francisco harbor. It had all started in the engine room, but by the time anyone realized something was wrong, men could be seen running down the deck, writhing and throwing themselves overboard in a futile attempt to extinguish the flames that had engulfed them all.

Jake frowned and growled. "They give us copper hammers so we won't create any sparks, and they take away our papers if we smoke on deck, and then they go and start a fire in the tanks."

On the final morning of tank welding, Charlie and the first

engineer came down into my tank to put the finishing touches on the crack. The First looked around the tank in wonderment. On the bulkhead by the crack, I had sketched with my fingers classic pirate scenes in the caked layers of oil that clung to the steel. I could see in his eyes that he felt as though he'd entered the cell of a prisoner who had been locked up in the Bastille just a little too long.

The violence of the welding, when I finally saw it up close, amazed me. The blue gas flame sent a cascade of sparks out in a six-foot radius. When I ran up to stamp out the smoldering bits of metal, the engineer held me back and told me not to worry about them. Then he casually stepped on a few of the larger coals nearest him, seemingly as an afterthought. His apparent coolness was augmented by his smoking a cigarette in the tank. Charlie may not have cared, wanting to establish an in with his superior (and so minimize his hassles); I, on the other hand, was shocked, but was in no position to start telling a longtime seaman—let alone an officer—how to conduct himself on a ship. But before we were done, when I found myself alone in the tank, I did take out my silent revenge on Texaco and the Seven Sisters by pissing in the tank, hoping that somewhere, six months later, some stockholder's Cadillac wouldn't start as a result.

CHAPTER 7

ONCE THE TANK HAD BEEN WELDED and sealed up, life on the *Rose City* returned to normal. There was still another week of Butterworthing to do before we reached Cabinda, but that was all routine now, and the Bosun assigned a number of lesser tasks in addition.

During the second weekend we took a break from Butterworthing and set about putting the final touches on the securing of the ship. Taking Billy and me up to the foredeck, the Bosun concocted a batch of black paint out of diesel crude and fish oil. With this syrupy tarlike brew he had the two of us paint the anchor blocks and fore winches until they sparkled. They did look great for the better part of a week. Then it rained and the Bosun's brew washed off, running down the deck in great streams, permanently staining everything it chanced to cross.

But we didn't care. As Billy put it, "I wouldn't mind swinging a paintbrush for a while—it'd beat the hell outta pushing those goddamn Butterworth machines around!"

Indeed, painting was soon the preferred job on the ship. Out in the cool sea air and the bright sun I could casually slap on the paint and turn my mind off. Nonetheless, even at this menial task I could do no right.

"You don't have to be no Rembrandt," the Bosun yelled at me when he noticed my attention to detail in painting the starboard winch. He said it in his friendly, almost fatherly way, but Billy, Bud, and the rest of the crew overheard the remark, and I didn't hear the end of it for a month and a half. If I could just gut it out till we reached Japan I'd be all right. Until then I hadn't much of a choice.

Billy's anger was often compounded by isolated incidents. Like any man on the edge, he could be ticked off by something as trivial as my feet on the coffee table. At one point I had borrowed Jake's Scotch tape and promptly misplaced it. Jake, never satisfied with anything anyway, was immediately disgusted with me. I turned to Billy in a moment of panic and asked him if he might not have borrowed it out of my room. He stared at me in shock and then, enraged, said, No, he hadn't taken the goddamn Scotch tape.

It sounds like an absurdist tragicomedy in retrospect, but at the time the incident was symptomatic of the tension among the three of us. Jake felt betrayed by me, and my carelessness served to confirm this. Billy, a paranoid in the true sense of the word, could not believe I had implicated him, drawing him into the arena of suspects. He later cornered me in the corridor and, fencing with his index finger, quietly warned me never to do that again or he'd do something violent. I was beginning to see an unpleasant pattern forming. As each day passed, I would directly or indirectly step on someone's toes. Each time I did I'd learn a little more about life on a ship. It also condemned me to further abuse. I was starting to realize the absolute need to mind my own bloody business. What you or anyone else was up to was the individual's concern alone. If you got into a beef with someone, no one else was going to even consider sticking his neck out for you. That was the way of the sea; on shore it was a different matter.

The razzing went on and on: From the hat I was wearing to my complete ignorance of the technical jargon, I was a pathetic joke. But there were moments when I was able to keep myself from wallowing in self-pity or fearing for my physical well-being. While painting the foredeck I got to know Tony for the first time.

It was just Tony, Jake, and me on the bow. There was a decidedly more relaxed atmosphere in the absence of the others. Jake was able to return somewhat to his role as my mentor, and Tony no longer played the role of the Silent Giant. Our friendship began simply enough, with casual conversation as we painted. Unlike the others', Tony's tone was inquisitive, not antagonistic. I'd respond frankly enough to his questions about my background without the usual fear of abuse and insult. It soon became clear that Tony himself was no ordinary seaman.

He had originally started as a crew member on seagoing tugs running between West Coast ports and Alaska. Yet while he'd speak of the usual adventures at sea—being caught in raging storms or seeing his best friend cut in half by a snapping cable—he'd also go into long discussions of his love for wine or his last stay in New Zealand. It seems he was simply unable to follow the straight and narrow course, and preferred a life of unknown possibilities.

Our friendship was confirmed by the chance coincidence that his cousin, while a grad student at Harvard, had rented an apartment from a very close friend of our family. Jake looked up now and then, occasionally firing a joke or two into the conversation, but he was clearly skeptical of the whole thing. It made no difference, as Tony was not only a confirmed seaman, he was the biggest man on the ship.

Once we were off work duty, though, Tony would disappear, and I was again left to my own devices. It's not just their isolation from civilization and their wives that causes seamen to be such a lonely lot—it's also their isolation from one another.

On June 26 we crossed the equator almost exactly at 0° latitude, 0° longitude. The second mate, whose job it was to plot our course, didn't have the imagination to steer us half a degree to the east so the crossing would be exact. A day or two later, while on watch, he realized he could've done it, and giggled moronically. No matter, really; I was happy just to have crossed the equator in a ship. Now I could get that gold earring in my left lobe, according to the old pirate tradition. (The right lobe signified you'd been in a shipwreck.)

Having crossed the equator also meant we were very close to arrival in Cabinda. I looked closely at the map of the world in the mess just to see where exactly Cabinda was, anyway.

A small nation on the lower west coast of Africa, Cabinda is separated from its parent country, Angola, by a

3"   June 26th

Dear Ma & Pa:

well, I don't Really have much to say for
myself. We're sailing off the coast of
Africa and headed for Angola of all
places to pick up a load of oil which
we will take to Japan. From
there we're supposed to hit Singapore
for Bunkers (fuel) and get another
load in Indonesia. I don't know
what then, probably Calf. where
I'll fly back, but it could be
Tunisia.

     I'm taking today off, in
other words I'm only doing
my regular watch (not
working overtime. 4 to 8 am
and then again 4 to 8 pm
7 days a week. I've been
generally working 16 hour days
since I got on board.

thin strip of land belonging to Zaire (thus affording it access to the sea). A former Portuguese colony, the tiny nation, because of its associations with Angola, had been taken over by the Cubans. But business is business, and while we may not have had any diplomatic recognition of the ruling government, their oil was very much on the minds of American corporations.

Morning lookouts were lasting longer now that we were in the tropical zone. Daylight saving time and the summer season had kept our watch light enough so that lookout was unnecessary for the most part. Alas, we were headed south, and as the days grew shorter, the lookouts grew longer. By the time we reached Cabinda, on the morning of June 28, it was still almost completely dark at six a.m.

Six a.m. was also the hour the Chief called all hands to make ready for docking. The day before, we had struggled over the damn gangway again, this time putting it back on the side of the ship even though we were cruising at 16 knots. Any one of the crew could've fallen overboard given an unexpected lurch. Now it was time to break out the lines once again and prepare to drop anchor.

We began on the stern. Stepping out onto the main deck, I was surprised to find it was suddenly light out. The orange glow of the dawn illuminated the mirrorlike surface of the sea and filled the sky with a soft pastel glow.

The crew was excited to go ashore at last, even if it was, in their view, "a shit port." The Bosun came up to me at one point and began sniffing the air, explaining that there was a different quality in the air as you approached land. As for the rest of the crew, their only thoughts were on the whores and the liquor they were dying for.

Then there was the discussion of how we were going to get ashore. The word had come down from the bridge that the company would not supply us with a launch to go back and forth from the ship (which would be moored a mile offshore, pumping the oil from "submarine" lines floated out from the refinery) and that visitors were discouraged. It was up to us, then, to contract a local sailor to ferry us ashore. It was a typical move on the part of the Captain: Do the absolute minimum for the crew; or, in other words, make a show at abiding by the union contract, and then make like the rest was out of his hands.

Billy led the forum on the logistics of the evening's party-

ing. He pointed out everyone in the room (carefully omitting me) and assigned them not a job but a state of drunkenness into which the assigned was to indulge. One of the boys was a cadet, an officer trainee from the Massachusetts Merchant Marine Academy. He was still a kid in many respects and shared the energy and attitudes of "the boys." Not yet an officer, but still a cut above the riffraff. Billy accepted him as a cast member anyway.

There was work to be done first, and the Bosun set to breaking out the lines. As usual, he worked the winch. There was no objection to this; not only was his heart weak, the bosun of a ship didn't have to go out on deck at all if he didn't want to, and most didn't. Dave Martin was a notable exception to this rule.

As we labored and the day grew lighter, small ships could be seen where there had been none only hours before. One such vessel pulled up alongside and, via a shaky rope ladder, our pilot climbed aboard. The pilot's job is the most elite in the Merchant Marine, his rank exceeding that of captain. The pilot's test was a very simple one, as Tony (whose ambition it was to become one) explained to me: They give you a blank map of the harbor you're testing for, and you have to fill in every depth, hazard, tide, time, and temperature that affects the region. Understandably, pilots were treated with deference when welcomed aboard, and were often presented with a number of gifts (especially pilots from Third World countries), which the captain had in waiting for just such occasions. A well treated pilot meant a quick and safe passage into the harbor and a good word to the customs officials. Our captain, however, didn't like the practice of giving away company property and gave a skimpy gift to the Angola pilot, who was understandably insulted by this miserliness. The pilot had to specifically ask for cigarettes and the like, and when our gracious captain refused we immediately gained a bad reputation in port.

And the work went on. I was glad to find the hauling of the lines was not killing me, as it had on the first night. Out of the

blue Tony turned to me and said I was doing "a real good job."
He also told me to slow down a bit and work in stages or I'd
burn myself out and start hurting. I was amazed; it was the first
encouraging thing I'd heard since I'd boarded the ship.

I looked up from the work at one point and suddenly realized we were surrounded by offshore oil rigs. It was no small
wonder why the Cubans were liberating Angola: This particular oppressed nation was fabulously rich in "black gold." The
rigs dotted the horizon as far as one could see, looking almost
like toys. As we made our way through this maze of rigs, they
grew in number. Each rig, suspended above the sea by what
seemed impossibly slender support beams, let off a dark oily
trail of smoke from its tower. Great tongues of flame licked the
sky as they burned off the deadly vapors that came up with the
crude, a grim reminder of our recent folly in the tanks.

Then I saw it: the hazy green-gray coast of Africa, at last
within our reach. Past the multimillion-dollar oil complexes,
where the local tribes beat out Agrico, and mercenaries could
stake out entire lands for their own.

The lines broken out, we turned in for breakfast. Before
long the Bosun called me. As an ordinary and the man with
least seniority, I was to go out with him to the bow and drop
anchor. In the then silvery morning—before the hot equatorial
sun had a chance to burn off the night's mist—we stood in the
quiet wind. The ship slowed down and came to a halt. The
Chief joined us with his walkie-talkie and leaned circumspectly
on the rail. As always there was the threat that the Captain
would be watching from the bridge.

As was his way, the Bosun explained in detail the process of
dropping anchor. When the word comes down from the bridge

you pull the pin, a weighty, two-foot bar of hardened iron, and let the chain drop a specific number of "cholks" (units), depending on how hard the current and how deep the water. Each cholk is ninety feet, the link that marks the end of a cholk being clearly painted in white. When the pin is pulled the chain whips down the hawse pipe with awesome force and speed.

The sun rose hot and bright. The tropical air shimmered with a buzz across the bay. We could barely make out the buildings on the shore a good mile away. If we were going into town tonight we were going to have a hard time of it; we could also make out the barbed-wire fences and pillboxes of the Cuban soldiers who strutted up and down the docks with regimental precision.

Upon our arrival we were greeted by both the government and the oil company. The government's hello was in the form of two fighter bombers that jetted over us on a number of passes and a helicopter that circled overhead as we pulled into the bay. The oil company sent over an expensive European-made launch filled with Portuguese executives and their entourage of natives from every former Portuguese possession except Angola. Shrewd politicking, no doubt.

For some reason the executives didn't trust the gangway and preferred to climb the thirty feet to the deck up the rickety rope ladder the pilot had come aboard on. Thus it was twenty minutes before the first exec gained the deck and greeted the Chief. The Captain awaited them in the air-conditioned bridge, where they soon retired.

The Africans were another story altogether. Unlike their bosses, who dressed in polyester leisure shirts and patent-leather loafers, they coveted their American blue jeans and T-shirts.

The T-shirt, however, had to say something on it. It didn't matter if it read PROPERTY OF THE DALLAS COWGIRLS or NUKE THE WHALES, so long as the slogan distinguished the shirt as a genuine American product.

The next step in the docking procedure was raising the submarine line and hooking it up to the manifold. The hard work was only just beginning.

As I've mentioned before, our equipment was primitive at best. The boom had to swing out over the side of the ship and drop so the cable and hook attached to the winch (the only mechanization) could reach the workers who waited by the pipeline in a boat below. Once they managed to secure the line to the hook, the winch slowly labored to raise it up to the level of the manifold. This was all relatively simple enough, but there was then the problem of bringing the pipeline to the manifold and hooking it up. While we tugged away at the boom, the Africans tried pulling the pipeline into the ship by a series of complicated ropeworks that ended up having little or no effect.

The main difficulty was our trouble communicating with the workers. The only word we had in common was *amigo*. They knew no English, and we knew no Portuguese. As a result, it ended up taking us two very long and grueling hours to hook everything up. This added to the crews' already simmering tempers, and there was a second line to hook up. Fortunately for all involved, this was accomplished in less than half an hour. We seemed to have figured out a system.

Our work done for the moment—the engine room and Spider the Pumpman taking over now that all systems were go—

we took a break, staring out at the town we feared we would never reach. I sat on the port rail and soaked up the sun.

Billy, who was walking around with a particularly angry look on his face, noticed me and yelled at me to get down. I looked at him and mumbled that I was only sitting on the railing. I thought to myself, *What the fuck is he giving me such a goddamn hard time for?*

"Did you ever hear of something called a ground swell? When you're in shallow water the ship could list violently, and you'd fall off and bust your fucking head!"

He turned his rage away from me after a while and started talking to the others about the vodka he was looking forward to on shore that night, and the party they were going to have. I got off the railing, trying to keep my cool. He was right. He was also being a bastard about it.

As the oil filled the tanks it was time to open the black market for business. Those workers who didn't have any immediate duties began plying us for our jeans, T-shirts, cigarettes, and, most important, our *Playboys*. In exchange they offered various trinkets from the countryside, or so they said. To me it looked like your basic hotel tourist fare. Ivory amulets and figurines, ebony and other wood carvings that had an oddly oriental look about them, and other junk. I was tempted to pick up something. The Chief had paid us all an allotment prior to our arrival in case we did get ashore, and the money was burning a hole in everybody's pocket.

As it turned out, the most desirable item they had to offer was pot. One of the workers, who spoke more English than the rest, approached me with a confidential air behind the

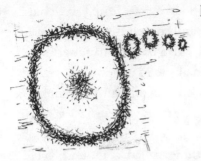

house. Wondering what was up, I pursued the conversation, and yes, in fact, he was selling marijuana. Despite my fear of being thrown into an Angola death pit, the romance of the situation was too much to miss out on, and I agreed to buy half an ounce of rich green grass from the heart of the Congolese jungle for ten bucks. We agreed to meet in fifteen minutes in the laundry room, where the switch was to be made. I was also to give him a *Playboy* and as many T-shirts as I had.

I nervously made my way back to my cabin. Throughout the house the workers were scouring every nook and cranny for everything they could find, flitting around with garbage bags full of soap, sheets, towels, magazines, and whatever else they could get their hands on. Anything that had been left out prior to docking was gone in a matter of minutes.

In my room I secured the money and picked out a couple of T-shirts and a *Penthouse*. Locking my door, something I did anyway, I made my way down to the laundry room. It was not so much the Angolan authorities that worried me; it was the rest of the crew. I already had to cut my hair because it was too long for the likes of the crew, but if they found out I smoked pot I was probably in serious trouble.

My man was there at the appointed time and place. We greeted each other in hushed tones and waited until we were sure all was clear. When we were both sure, I pulled out my ten dollars and handed him a plastic bag that contained the shirts, some soap and towels, and the magazine. He looked at the merchandise with care. It looked bad for a moment; he wanted more. I held my ground: This was my turf, and I had what he wanted. As for the pot, I could take it or leave it. He stared coolly into my eyes, betraying no sense of treachery, and then slowly reached into his cheap pseudo-European-style bell-bottoms (circa 1967) and pulled out a fist-size bundle of newspaper. He opened it up, and there was the stuff. I eyeballed it carefully—this joker had better not try to pull a fast one. It seemed legit, and the deal was made. I made my way back upstairs to my room and stashed the stuff in the ventilation system above my bed. Outside, in the hall, the Bosun was bitching that someone had left the linen closet open and half the sheets had been lifted.

As the day wore on it became clear we weren't going to get ashore. My one attempt at getting through to the fellow who spoke at least some English failed utterly. He somehow thought that the boat and liquor I was describing were for his mates and himself so they could come aboard that night and have a party at our expense. Although Miguel later came forward to act as our interpreter, there was no chance of gaining passage ashore. The Cubans had seen to that.

One fellow did manage to go into town. A QMED, he had intended to stay on, or so he said, for a year in order to make big bucks. But midway through the second week on board he found he had developed a hernia and had to see a doctor.

He was a particularly odd bird, this one. Standing about six-four in height, he had shaved his head but not his beard, in order to be more comfortable while working in the searing heat of the engine room. This lent him an appearance like that of Charles Manson, which he cultivated by loping grimly around the lounge with a twisted look in his eye, calmly cooing, "Charlie's waiting for you."

The rest of the crew silently watched him, having no doubts that he was an oddball, one to be generally ignored.

On the few occasions I had a chance to talk with him he turned out to be very cool. Like Charlie, he was a patchwork of multicolored tattoos, but he also sported a gold earring in his left lobe. Clearly a former hippie, he talked about smuggling pounds of pot into the States by means he did not care to divulge. He did speak on one occasion of a time when he'd dropped several pounds of hashish over the side prior to a customs inspection. He obviously enjoyed the risk; he had a singular smile on his face as he told the story, the smile worn by mercenaries, revolutionaries, and negotiators who thrive on screwing the other guy.

As he was waiting to go ashore there arose another general discussion on the prospect of leaving the ship. Billy wanted booze, Charlie wanted chicks, and everyone else wanted off to have a wild time. When it was generally agreed there was no hope of shore leave, Billy turned to me in his spiteful, mocking way and told me I should "get [my] daddy to phone someone and get us ashore."

I looked at him and frowned. Almost whiningly I retorted that he couldn't do a damn thing, and who'd he think my father was, anyway? God Almighty?

Actually, I didn't say it in so many words at all. Even so, I was very tired of having him bait me in front of the rest of the crew, then sit back smiling while I squirmed helplessly. Just then the QMED spoke up and told the gathered crew to "leave the kid alone. He's gotta make his bread, too." The mocking stopped, and I suddenly had an ally.

Naturally this new balance couldn't last for long, and when the QMED was taken ashore in the launch, life returned to normal. Billy strutted into the lounge and informed us that there was a whole new angle to our nixed visit to Cabinda: me. Apparently the Old Man was scared like hell that as a senator's son I was a potential political target. My strong desire to go ashore—something he couldn't stop if we found a boat that would take us—might result in the Cubans discovering my identity and kidnapping me.

At this I groaned. Billy told me it was no joke. And to myself I cursed, and wished like hell they would all go and fuck themselves.

Being able to take no more, I left the lounge and went off to bed. As I went through the door that closed off the stairwell from B deck, Spider, the small Indonesian pumpman, called me into his room. I had made his acquaintance by giving him a Djarum, he having been born in Sumatra and raised on clove cigarettes. Now it seemed he was returning the favor.

Out of his desk drawer he pulled a familiar-looking wad of newspaper. When he opened it, the room was instantly filled with the pungent aroma of fresh marijuana. I was delighted; now at least I wasn't the only one with dope on the ship. Shoving a towel against the crack at the bottom of the door, Spider proceeded to roll and light a joint. I felt as if I were back in high school, sneaking a high and hoping I wouldn't get caught.

CHAPTER 8

A S USUAL, the 12–4 watch woke me up at 3:20, always
an hour short of a good night's sleep. Coming into
the lounge for the prerequisite cup of coffee, I heard one of
the workers excitedly trying to explain that his partner had
smashed open his head. I made my way down to the main
deck and into the infirmary room, where the Second was leaning over a sullen-looking African and cutting away at his hair
with a pair of scissors. Several other workers, on duty oversee-
ing the pumping by the manifold, stood about, inspecting the
progress of the operation. The blood that streamed down from
the man's skull and over the side of his face apparently came
from a wound received when the oil fumes got the better of
him and he passed out and cracked his head on the hard metal
deck. When we all heard the story, Africans and seamen alike
looked at the poor injured fellow with disbelief. We had all
been out there and none of us had experienced symptoms of
this nature, let alone even begun to find the fumes oppressive;
yet there he was, with his head split open, in the quiet African
night, getting a haircut from an obese American officer who
had rudimentary training in first aid.

Following this odd interlude, I went out to the manifold to stand port watch. Unlike sea watch, only one man at a time was required to be on duty when the ship was at anchor, a token gesture of vigilance.

The sun seemed somehow larger along the equator. Red and swollen, it rose languidly over the African continent as the watch slowly passed. Gradually I was able to strike up a conversation with the worker from whom I'd bought the pot the day before. Although he nodded and gestured like any number of foreigners when approached by confused American tourists who think that if they talk slowly and loudly enough they will be understood, he relaxed and carried his part of the conversation.

He was from the Ivory Coast. He was fortunate to have such a well-paying job, but he still lived in the shadow of the Portuguese oil execs, who treated him like a servant or even a slave. It was a situation much like what I'd seen in India in the early '70s: a labor-intensive economy where ninety percent of the population lived on the brink of complete desperation. Those who had jobs were in no position to question the motivations or actions of their employers. I glanced up at the bridge for a moment before returning to our conversation.

When the topic of the conquering Cuban army arose, his voice gained a new urgency. He may not have been a native Angolan, but the threat of a new wave of colonialism colored his words. Less than thirty miles from where we were anchored, there was intense fighting going on between the Cuban forces and the Angolan guerillas. Resistance was nominal in that there was a massive famine throughout the countryside decimating the population, the result of the Cubans' culinary taste.

"Tongue of cow" is a great delicacy in Cuba, and upon arrival the Cuban soldiers promptly set about shooting all the native cattle and cutting out the tongues for an evening's repast. Not only were the Angolans not allowed to eat the carcasses, but the extinction of their most vital food and energy source had initiated the famine that now swept the country.

Meanwhile, on the shore the rigid figures of the liberators continued to march back and forth along the docks.

The QMED returned from his foray to the mainland with the news that he had a hernia and was unqualified to work and was eligible to be flown home by the company. Although he would lose lots of overtime, he would be paid his flat rate for as long as the *Rose City* was at sea on this particular voyage. The hernia was supposedly acquired while performing his duty for the company, so he was within his rights to claim his full health benefits as guaranteed by the union contract. He had it made in the shade.

This turn of events cast a number of things in a new light. First, we were now going to be able to give him letters to mail for us upon his return to the United States. I hadn't been able to write or cable my parents since the ship's orders had been changed, and I felt it was probably a good idea to keep my mother from having a stroke when I failed to return home on time. Second, it meant that the engine crew was now reduced to three men, and Spider, the pumpman, would be forced to do double duty, taking up the vacated watch. It also meant I'd lost my only ally.

Before he left I took him aside and up to my room. In a secretive manner I unscrewed the overhead vent and pulled out my pot. He watched the procedure sardonically, explaining that the vent was the first place the customs people would look in my room. The idea is to stash any contraband you might have (which often includes pornography, especially in Arab countries known for their outrageous fines) in a neutral spot like the engine room or the forepeak. If they found something there they could only fine the ship itself, and not bust any individual. It was good advice from someone who knew the ropes, and I took it to heart. I doled out several joints' worth and, wrapping it up in an envelope, handed it to him. He was most appreciative and promised to mail my letters promptly, which, as it turns out, he did.

It was too bad that he had to go. Miguel prepared some sandwiches to hold him over during his wait in Cabinda before his flight out. As his launch sped toward the mainland it looked like he was off to a long, lonely exile in some godforsaken jungle dictatorship.

Speculation on his character arose immediately upon his departure. No one, it was realized, had ever seen him in the union hall. Pete pointed out that he hadn't been able to carry his own bags up the gangway when we boarded at Eagle Point, which was odd for a fellow that big. Then it dawned on us that he had developed the hernia before he'd even boarded the ship and had played his cards perfectly. Not mentioning his condition to anyone, he'd signed up for the longest job he could find, making like he was ready to stay on for a year (right down to the shaving of his head). In the second week of hard work he "was injured" and got off at the first port and was flown home at the company's expense. While we slaved away at sailing around the world, he'd be sitting at home collecting a parallel pay. I didn't begrudge the guy, but the rest of the crew thought he was a louse.

The last we ever heard of him was sometime later. The Angolan authorities, so Sparks informed us, had delayed his flight
for upward of a week and held him in some unknown border
station. On hearing this, the Bosun was outraged and raised a
general outcry among crew members against the negligence of
the company. I mentioned this to the Chief while on watch one
morning. He snickered. The Chief, too, knew that the QMED
had conned the company into a free ride, and didn't care if he
rotted in Africa for a month. Officers were, as Jake explained,
"company men."

In all we were in Cabinda for less than twenty-eight hours.
By four p.m. on the second day we were letting go for the next
leg of the journey: down under Africa, around the Cape of
Good Hope, through the Indian Ocean, and up to Japan by
way of the Straits of Malacca. As part of their "energy saving"
policy, the company ordered us to reduce speed to 13 knots.
This was the worst news the crew had heard so far, and by
far the most dispiriting. Traveling at 13 knots meant that we
wouldn't reach Japan until August, thirty-three days hence.
The claustrophobia sank in even deeper, and the *Rose City* became a very quiet ship indeed.

The boys were still hungover from a beer party they'd had
the night before and were shuffling around the house in an
angry or depressed state. Having had no part of it, I simply
went about my duties and remained as much in the background as possible. Then Joe entered
the picture.

Crusty like the other old-timers,
his job as the 12–4 ordinary called
upon him to sugie (swab) B deck and

the stairwell in the afternoons. I was leaving for p.m. overtime when he told me to leave my door unlocked so he could give my room the once-over with the mop. He was quite forceful in his tone of voice, and I was intimidated into relenting. I went to work with an uneasy feeling in my gut; I'd left the pot in my desk drawer.

Sure enough, at dinner the Bos made reference to Joe's snooping activities. That was almost my breaking point. My cabin was the one place on the ship where I could hold on to my identity and escape the continual razzing and the back-breaking pressure of the job. Now in a flash all that was gone, and they had one more thing on me. Thus, evening watch over with, I closed myself up in my room and drank the better part of my week's ration of beer. Dark and silent, the room at least continued to provide temporary shelter.

There were more than thirty days to go. No two ways about it, no bailing out of the job because the work was unpleasant, no dropping the class because the teacher didn't like me.

I had been lost in the turmoil of settling in to the drama. Now everything was set. The players knew their parts, and there wasn't going to be a scene change for a long time to come.

I turned to my journal.

I've thought up a war scenario, but I can't write it just now, for I've realized that Joe has probably pored over the contents of my room. Today the Bos at dinner welcomed Joe saying, "Ah, here's Joe, the house detective," and earlier, while on sanitary duty, Joe had told me, "Leave your door open, I'll clean your room."

I'm in something deeper than I thought . . . The crew's levels
of intermixture . . . I'm in such an open position that I have to
watch my fucking step.
The Eight of Wands INVERTED! Ah, yes, the dream.
It was there!
The dream
The room search
The sea
The void: The void is lost in the paranoia suddenly,
crashing in on and convulsing my situation out here alone
on a ship of tough salts and so seemingly vulnerable.
Nothing is an issue
Anymore.

—6/22/80

The void is the center of the Taoist religion. It is the primal
serenity whence we spring, and into which meditators return.
Through my wanderings in the East and my embracing of the
counterculture, I attempted to adopt this perspective as my own.
This cryptic entry in my journal refers to my agitated emotional
state as I lost touch with this Eastern calmness. The entry was
made (and amply annotated with frantic drawings) on the evening of our first full day at sea since letting go in Cabinda.

The next few days were relatively uneventful. On overtime I
got to know Tony better and established the makings of a good
rapport. He was smart, had a macabre sense of humor, and was
prone to crazed acts of buffoonery.

The Atlantic was uncharacteristically calm, the weather cool and sunny. It was a strange new sensation to go out on deck for overtime. The ship was now fully laden, and the main deck rested only eight feet above the waterline. Cutting smoothly through these peaceful waters was one thing, but every now and then a large swell would wash up over the railing and swamp the deck. And choppy waters were bound to hit when we rounded the Cape.

It was also clear that we were headed south. After gutting out yet another horrendous New England winter, I was more than ready for the hot summer months. It was a cruel act of poetic justice that put me on a ship that was destined for the lower hemisphere. Lookouts were getting colder by the day, and before long we were in the midst of yet another freezing winter season.

In the house, the crew was in a state of emotional hibernation. Each morning at 3:20 when the watch woke us and Billy, Jake, and I would sleepily struggle down to the lounge, Billy would pace into the lounge and, shifting his tired bones into one of the chairs, with a saturnine grin pronounce the number of days left to go. But that was it. To think about the weeks ahead was to go insane. We'd watch movies, read books, or talk about the day's work and weather, but not about the trip. There was talk about the union hall, and characters from Philly, but not about the wives and girlfriends. Not yet, anyway; that was too far away, and far too painful.

And so the time passed. Resigned to the fact that even the kindly Bosun might turn on me for having pot, and suppressing my fear of being thrown overboard or getting punched out, I went about living day by day. Off in the great expanse of the ocean I watched for omens. One day whales, the next day an albatross, and so on. In the evening I'd take in the sunset, letting the dark forms of the playing porpoises lull me into a quiet trance.

July 4 was in many ways a turning point. As it came on a Friday, we were now privileged to one of those happy coincidences that gladdens even the saltiest of hearts: *premium weekend.* Because it was a federal holiday we were working overtime and could collect top wages. In my case that was $7.67 an hour. Dollar signs rang up in everybody's eyes.

The day began with Jimmy waking me up for watch. I'd rapped with him a few times in the lounge, and his soft-spoken Philly twang had none of the antagonism of the others'. After he'd given me the watch report, he got almost excited (torpidity was a natural way with him). The ship was rounding the Cape, and off the port beam the lights of Cape Town were filling the night sky.

I was too tired to jump right out of bed, despite my better judgment. The point of this trip was, after all, to take in as many different phenomena as possible. But like the others, I was becoming nonchalant in my attitude. This was not to last long. Stepping out on the port wing to relieve Bud, I saw what Jimmy was talking about: The great dormant mass of the African continent was suddenly alive with the great spectacle of Cape Town. We were so close to the coast I could practically make out the broad avenues that ran through the town. It was a brilliant light show.

Inside the bridge the Chief and the Old Man were running around in an attempt to navigate the ship along the proper sea channel. One of the busiest spots in the ocean, the Cape of Good Hope was alive with seagoing vessels of all sorts and nationalities.

My reverie was cut short by the Chief's orders to keep an eye out for a crucial lighthouse and any new lights. I was more than happy to oblige: This was the turning point to warmer waters. From here on out we were headed north, and the African winter—along with those freezing winds that made lookout a misery—was soon to be left behind.

On overtime, Jake, Tony, and I sugied the stack deck. I was feeling a bit more cheerful, mellowing into the situation, keeping the spirit up. It was becoming a ritual for the three of us to work overtime together. Our conversation consisted of sea stories, Jake's politicking, and Tony's singing. As it turned out, Tony was an accomplished banjo player and would regularly break into a goofy rendition of any number of songs. As if illustrating the lightness of mood in which the three of us worked, a gooney bird (as Bud called them) hovered three feet over Jake and Tony for several minutes without their knowing.

In the evening I calculated my earnings to date and came up with a figure of around $2,000. It dawned on me that I was going to make lots of money. I filled out the day's overtime and sat back on my bed. On the bedside shelf I'd put all the books I'd brought along to read. Collecting dust were unopened volumes of *Lord Jim, The Reivers,* and *Seven Arrows.* I reached out to the end of the shelf and picked up the Penguin edition of *Moby-Dick.*

The day started after a night of wild dreams. On watch I had a lot of fun spotting boats while we circled around, mea-

suring the compass against a light on what are the southern mountains of Africa. The dark birds, later on OT, were hassling the seagulls on and off. It was a beautiful day, morning especially, as the sea was a rolling, lolling mirror. The sun hung low and twilightish all day. Billy continued his violent hot and cold. I thought I saw a bird floating in the water as we sailed along. Lots of shit otherwise in the bend of the Cape of Good Hope. We splashed fish oil around, and as I ascended the wheel—a gorgeous sunset on the smooth rippled sea, and a wonderful view of the southernmost plains-mountains of Africa—sigh—. I saw the cadet again today, watching the sunset. But the key was when I relieved Jake on watch—ah, the sea sparkled with an incredible violet-green illumination. As we plunged through the steadily warmer waters the ship churned up glowing plankton—what a trip!

—7/5/80

It was true: The sea off the Cape was awash in trash. Everything from oil spills to kitchen garbage could be seen floating idly in the usually turbulent waters. And for this we were lucky—the Cape is generally known for its violent winter storms. It was assumed that this was where I'd experience my first bout with seasickness, but this was not to be. The weather was perfect, the sailing smooth. Smooth enough to see the death of this picturesque channel.

The phosphorescent sea was the most startling thing I'd seen. It was still light out when I came off the wheel, and it seemed as if this was going to be just another evening watch. It was dark when I came on lookout. It was not just another evening watch. The great wake stirred up by the ship had vast, glowing repercussions throughout the dark sea. Ten-foot waves of neon green buffeted the bow and ran angrily down the side of the ship and past the house. The view from the stern was no less magnificent. The great screw bubbled and sang in a symphony of light. Our path was marked out by a vibrant green line that shone in the darkness clear across the horizon.

When Joe relieved me he was duly unimpressed. He'd seen it before, and it was nothing to him. I stared down at the bow for a few minutes longer, and then decided I had to go out on the deck to the forepeak. This was not a good idea— and is one of the cardinal sins on a ship. Should a swell rise up and crush me against the pipes or knock me overboard there would be no one to help me, or even to hear my cries. Nonetheless, I had to go.

Walking out onto the long, imposing deck was not an easy thing to do. The house was a looming bastion of security and light, but the bow at night was dark and elemental. After a few minutes I reached the forepeak and braved the ladder to the foredeck. It was awesome. The phosphorous wave rose up and thundered against the ship. The water splashed across the deck and, receding, pulled back for another assault. Again great waves of light crashed into our iron hull, and again the ship plunged on. It was an epic battle.

Sunday was Billy's twenty-sixth birthday. I had made a birthday card with a pen rendering of a genie coming out of a bottle but couldn't think of a way to give it to him. Finally I decided to get it over with, and while at the wheel I stepped out onto the wing, where he was standing lookout, and handed it to him. He looked up surprised and silently accepted it. Later I heard that he really appreciated it, and I was glad.

On the outside, the dusky hills of South Africa were passing by, and the sea continued to be crowded with vessels. Part of the experience of going around the Cape was mastering the wheel. The course changed regularly as we made our way along the coast, and I was getting a handle on the mechanics of steering. At first I was shaky; a laden tanker has a hell of a momentum to it, and my first course change was a bit of a disaster. The Chief told me to swing ten degrees right. Taking her off the gyro, I made the usual course change. But the ship didn't stop. Panicking, I pulled her hard left, and she finally responded. Unfortunately she was again pulling much harder than I'd expected, and I jerked the wheel fast the other way. After five minutes or so she was finally on course, and, flipping the gyro

switch, I returned the controls to automatic. The Chief in the meantime had been watching my struggle with an amused look on his face.

"When a ship's laden, you've got to compensate for it. Say you've got to take her fifteen degrees left. When you see that she's at seven or so, pull her fast thirty degrees right. That'll balance 'er out and get her under control."

All things considered, the Chief was all right. While at the wheel he'd shoot the breeze with me about this or that, often using me to vent his feelings about the crew or the way work was going. For my part, I picked his brain about the sea. While the crew had an intuitive understanding of the ocean, he had a scientific knowledge. It was good background; his talks on the technicalities of the Merchant Marine also helped me pass the long hours on watch.

Even so, he still continued to call the crew "a bunch of dumbshits."

The compulsion to be accepted was fear. Here it's a different world. It's closed. Real. Fair.

—7/6/80

Africa faded out over the horizon, a thick stretch of gray. We were in the Indian Ocean. Throwing the Tarot, I turned up the Tower. It made sense. I had gone from an overgrown playground where Westchester Marxists drove Daddy's car to the protest and conversation focused on feminism and boycotting Nestlé into a vengeful situation. Here the only escape was the eventual passage of time. I had reached the LCD. The pits. And then a curious thing started happening: I began to almost enjoy it. In the absolute still of the morning watch, in the rapt hour before the dawn when the only light was the dull glow of the electric compass and the useless pulsings of the broken radar, in the foaming seas of another hemisphere and on another side of the planet, I relished the thought that all those fuckers back there at the university were scratching one another's eyes out with the same old bullshit. There was none of that here. None you could get away with, anyway. This was life and death with every turn of the compass. It was real.

It was a strangely comforting thought.

On the seventh the clouds began to gather. Monsoon season, which I had once longed for, sweating out the blistering heat of India, now loomed with grave intensity, and we were sailing into the heart of it.

The Bosun had us chipping and scraping in preparation for a massive painting project the Chief had planned. On our return to the States, the Coast Guard was going to inspect the ship, and everything had to look smart. It didn't matter that it took twenty minutes to force the lifeboats out of their frozen moorings, or that the three compasses on the bridge all read different points. Just so long as everything looked nice.

Nothing much today. Slept in this morning and lazed into lunch and afternoon work. Blustery seas. Beautiful sunset—endless cumulus clouds illuminated various shades

*of red, lavender, and blue, iridescent against the electric
blue-green sky. Shocks of rays bolted out from behind a cloud
that calmly shielded us from the setting sun. They say a typhoon is expected. Billy's been a decent chap. Today.*

—7/7/80

*Taking strong seas on the starboard side. There was no OT
today.*

—7/8/80

As we entered the Indian Ocean, which had been described to
me as sweltering but peaceful, the ship was assaulted by barrage
after barrage of angry waves. It started out as a series of excep-
tionally large swells washing over the deck; soon, however, it
became clear that we were in the midst of the remnants of a
typhoon, and to leave the house was suicide. The view from
the bridge was the best. As the ship rode the waves, mountains
of water swept over the railing and crashed against the steam
pipes. Every tenth wave or so the entire deck, from starboard
to port side, was swamped. How long the storm was going to
last was uncertain. We had two weeks to go before the Straits,
and in this season there was the possibility that the bad weather
wouldn't abate even then. Through the rain-choked windows
one could see the ship's great iron hulk buckling under the
force of the storm, the entire ship convulsing in a series of rip-
ples that ran down the whole length of the deck.

Since there was no overtime to be had, the crew whiled away
the hours by drinking the last of the booze. The Heineken

the officers had been selling us ran out that week, and the liquor-starved seamen began a desperate hunt for the few remaining intoxicants left on the ship. One night Jake and Jimmy called me into Jake's room, where they were getting drunk on their last case. I brought in most of my own alcohol and proceeded to join them in a three-hour binge that left us trashed and in incredible pain for the next morning's watch.

It was a great evening. Jake, the character actor, provided nonstop entertainment for the two of us. Jimmy, for his part, told outrageous sea stories and terrible jokes. The highlight was when Jake broke out his harmonica and went into a rendition of Hitler's favorite jig. His seasoned face turned red as a beet as he tooted madly away, jumping up and down and laughing hysterically.

Jimmy, when he finally stopped laughing, recounted a story he'd heard from someone in the union hall about Jake. As he described it, Jake was in a hotel in Saigon with some of the boys when he found he had to go to the bathroom. Crossing the ballroom, lavishly decorated like some palace out of a Bing Crosby–Bob Hope *On the Road* picture, he suddenly leaped up onto the stage and broke into "On the Road to Mandalay."

Laughing, I remarked that I'd been to Mandalay while living in India. The two of them fell silent. I'd blown it. I'd reminded them of who I was, and our drunken comradeship was broken. Jimmy eventually lifted his head and uncomfortably looked away out the window.

"Y'know, it's not how much money you have," he said. "It's what you do with your life."

The party broke up soon after that.

Aside from reading *Moby-Dick* my only pastimes were the movies in the lounge. Occasionally I would sneak into the kitchen late at night and steal a can of whipped cream. Hiding it under my shirt, I'd make my way out onto the stack deck and slowly suck out the nitrous oxide (laughing gas) that propelled it. It was a cheap thrill, but then there weren't too many alternatives. It was very amusing to see the crew puzzling over why the whipped cream didn't work the next morning.

By the eighth, the booze was gone. Miguel and Ned started trying to brew raisin jack in the mess, but it was generally a dismal failure. Nonetheless, they, Billy, and a few of the others drank it. Rumor had it that the reason Miguel often locked himself in his room for long periods of time was to drink Listerene. Billy said he and a mate of his had done that at Piney Point, the training academy where no liquor was allowed. He also said that it made them sick to their stomachs, but it did get them drunk. Other tales of being caught without booze included the story of one seaman who when desperate for a drink, emptied the alcohol out of the compass and drank that. I mentioned this to the Chief, and he said, "Why not? It's pure, ain't it?"

The skies over the Indian Ocean are epic. With nothing but sea below them, they open up with cyclopean grandeur. The great storm clouds of the monsoon rise up and out without measure.

On the morning of the ninth I saw perhaps the most impressive example of this. As we sailed into the east, the bridge looked straight into the amber sun that rose over the hyperactive sea through restless, scattered storm clouds. Coming at us full force was a rain squall that, because of the sun behind it, appeared as a great sheet of glistening orange. Smoothly working its way across the water, it soon engulfed us. It didn't last more than a minute before moving on to the west, when I realized there was no rainbow. I stepped out onto the port wing and stopped. Filling the sky was a beautiful double circular rainbow, vivid and perfect. It plunged deep into the sea, and up again into the sky. Gradually it drifted off, borne away by the gray sheet of rain that receded into the horizon.

Something told me that this was an omen. After all, there were only twenty-four days to go.

Well, no work today; I feel like I'm unemployed. As for remarkable phenomena, I saw on the p.m. watch (port wing) the same flashes/sparkles I had observed earlier, except there were also great bursts of that same cool blue electric light, like flashbulbs going off under the surface of the onrushing water. Aye, 'twas odd; whole patches would light up.

—7/10/80

As a lark, one night I drew a picture of Jake as a rebel standing in front of the Confederate flag. That he would act like a "reb" sometimes had been a running joke for a few weeks now, one that Jake himself had laughed at. Seizing upon this, I taped the cartoon to his door and thought nothing more about it.

The next morning, Billy, with a smile on his face, asked me if I had done the drawing. When I told him I had he laughed and walked off. Jake was not so amused.

When we were both on the bridge at the same time we'd usually stand at the doorway—one on lookout, the other on the wheel—and shoot the breeze. He had a wealth of sea stories and a love of telling them. I was more than happy to lend an ear. But that night he was not so cheery. I was on the wheel when Jake came up for lookout. He said his usual curt hello to the Chief on his way through the bridge to the wing. The gloom of night obscured his features, but I could tell he was upset.

Standing way out on the wing, he kept to himself for half an hour. I finally decided to break the ice. Going up to the door, I got his attention, and he came slowly over. Though he was an old and tired little man, his body was still as tough as an ox's. He looked at me with that mixture of suspicion and betrayal tempered by his liking for me as his apprentice.

I told him I was sorry about the picture. It was intended as a friendly joke, but I guessed it was not in good taste.

He frowned. "That's okay. It's all right to joke about these things, but you can't pin a label on somebody. Out here there's something we call the Court Jester Syndrome. Y'know, like the clowns played for the king. When a fellow on a ship starts being treated like one, he can't shake it. It can build up on a ship. Tensions can flare and build up. You've gotta be careful what you say about the other guy. One time I was on this ship when we had a real performer. Patty Finn was his name. A little fella, but he had a real mean temper. One time this big guy starts giving him trouble in the mess, and before you know it they were humping on each other, and plates were flying. We crawled under the tables . . ."

And so on. Having made his point and illustrated it, he went back into his sea stories, laughing and gesturing, aping the characters with a professional's skill. I still hadn't cooled down enough. My propensity for overstepping the line, even at this advanced point in the trip and after all the railroading I'd already gotten, was still rearing its ugly head. I guess I'd hit a little too close to home.

But I was not the only subject of abuse. The old black steward's insistence on being woken up early, and his surly manner in the kitchen, soon made him a very unpopular character. He was an old-timer (i.e., he knew the ropes), so no one messed with him to his face. But when he wasn't around he was the subject of much angry derision. Billy was especially vehement in his attacks.

Billy had grown up in a bad part of town, working in gangs sometimes, stealing refrigerators or breaking into freight trains. His attitude toward blacks was partly the result of this background. The back-alley rivalry between the black and Irish gangs was no doubt very intense.

So it was that he hated the old steward. The others generally agreed—the old-timers especially. Dave Martin, as usual, was a remarkable exception to this rule. He seemed to give everybody a fair chance and judged them on their abilities, not on their backgrounds. There were a number of reasons for this. The first was that Dave had been the toughest seaman around since the '40s. He'd been known to deck a first mate and escape by swinging from the boom line off the ship and onto the dock, where a car was waiting. In his time he'd taken them all on, and because he usually won he didn't have the insecurities that drove others into fits of rage. On the other hand, Dave was also very close to death. A number of times he graphically recounted his stroke. It had left him weakened, but, as the old saying goes, unbowed; yet it had seriously affected his wild character. Almost tender at times, he now approached his crews with a good-natured, encouraging attitude. It sometimes drove the others crazy; they thought he was approaching senility. And his logic was often misguided. Once, when I suggested an easier way to go about a certain job, he looked up and said, "You're not paid to think."

And that was that. You couldn't change his mind, but you couldn't help liking him. His sea stories aside—of which he had by far the most and the best—you could listen to him for hours as he sang his ribald limericks and songs. It was one of the ways he kept the crew in a good mood, and their minds off the work and their homesickness.

His finest song:

> *For forty days and forty nights*
> *They sailed the broad Atlantic*
> *And on the shore they spied some whores*
> *And went into a panic.*

> *They partied hearty with those girls*
> *On that island off the map,*
> *But when the weeks went by, and they all set sail,*
> *They wound up with the clap.*

> *Of pain and misery each sailor he did talk,*
> *And wanted nothin' but the pain*
> *To leave 'is 'urting cock. . . .*

They were psychological chanties that kept the rhythm going.

Saturday the twelfth the seas had calmed down enough that we could go back out on deck. It was as if Mother Nature had given us a two-day reprieve so we could work overtime at the premium rate. A month had gone by, and in theory the trip was a third over.

The air was crystal, and the sun shone down warmly through the still chilly day. It was nice to get outside after four days inside. The Bosun put us to work cleaning up the rusted steam pipes with fish oil and scrapers. I worked the starboard side, Billy and Bud the port. That morning on watch the Chief had asked me to note the bearing of a ship that was passing us. When Billy came up to relieve me I told him that there was a ship bearing 120 degrees.

He looked at me and, scowling, said, "I don't give a fuck what the ship's bearing. What the fuck? That's not my job."

The crew was not responsible for navigation, so he used this as an excuse for another opportunity to give me more hell. Sure enough, as we fish-oiled he told Bud the story, and they both laughed.

After an hour a jet plane buzzed the ship.

"Hey, Monahan, what's it bearing?" Billy yelled.

I kept looking down but mumbled, "He's bearing his ass." Pretty pathetic, but it was the only thing I could think of at the time.

Billy turned to Bud. "What did he say?"

"He said, 'He's bearing his ass.' "

"Right, Monahan. You've got a long row to hoe. Yeah, a long row to hoe."

That became his motto, and he repeated it to me at least twice a day for the next three weeks.

In the same afternoon, we passed our first South Seas islands: Mauritius and Réunion. They were picture-perfect manifestations of the archetypal tropical paradises. Mauritius, the first one on our route, was a serene vision of lush forests covering the rolling hills, basking in a wash of soft rain clouds that obscured its uppermost peaks. I couldn't help idealizing it—it was too perfect. An island in the sun true to my dreams.

Watch the next morning was bizarre. On lookout I noticed an increase in the number of shooting stars. They aren't uncommon at sea, where the absence of lights and pollution brings out constellations you never knew were there. In the Southern Hemisphere it was even more spectacular, as the Southern Cross leads a host of celestial bodies not found in the heavens of the north. But that night there was a veritable shower of shooting stars. Then from out of the night a huge fiery meteorite exploded into view and crashed into the sea with a roar. There was an omen.

Later, when I took the wheel, the Old Man came up onto the bridge. He did this occasionally, sending the Chief into a nervous panic. I minded my own business, staring off vacantly, pretending not to listen to their conversation. Then the Old Man turned his attention to me.

"So how's the hippie business doing? You were born ten years behind your time."

I looked at him. What in the hell did he mean by that? He kept on with his monologue.

"They'll take all the fun out of pot when they legalize it," he said, and then made other references to San Francisco and Flower Power.

What was going on?

I was eventually relieved and went down to the lounge with an uneasy feeling. Even so, I couldn't help being amused by the Old Man's corny lines.

In the lounge there was only Miguel. Ned and Pete were in the kitchen, silently preparing breakfast. Miguel sat up in his chair and gave me a concerned look.

In a confidential tone he spoke to me.

"You know that big fat motherfucker Frank?" Frank was the other QMED, whom no one seemed to notice but his fellow old-timers. "The other day he come in here and see your coat on the hook there, and he grab it and throw it on the ground. If I knew you better I'd tell him to pick up the motherfucking coat or *pow!* Anyway, I thought you should know."

My stomach contracted at the news. Here we go again—new cast, same old program. Twenty days to go, twenty days to go . . .

Taking on seas once again. I slept in this morning, woke at noon and got usual shit from Billy, then worked in the passageway. Fixed the fluorescent lights in my room and restarted Gor. Ah, yes . . .

—7/14/80

Each day, I suppose, will get better, but for now I feel that real fear—claustrophobic helplessness. The paranoia that

threatens to seize me is for now unconsummated (may it
always be so), as no real harm has been done to me yet. Ver-
bal abuse reigns for now. I am alone and entrapped with no
friends and many enemies. Today Billy on watch came over to
the window and flipped me the finger and then began, but was
unable to finish, what startled me as a VERY SERIOUS repri-
mand for too much, or rather prolonged, clowning. "You can't
do that on a ship," etc., etc. It's a DEADLY serious business,
and I fear that I continue to step on people's toes. Granted, a
lot of the shit I get, especially from Billy, is because I'm green,
but more particularly because they know I won't, and can't,
talk/act back. The trouble is that in responding I all too
often hit many wrong chords so that the situation worsens.
Catch-22—damned if I do, and damned if I don't. I've got to
find a real neutral ground. They go out of their way to remind
me I am not like them . . . I am now dangerously alienated.
I'll have to assume that when Joe searched my room it made
me all the more open for their target practice. Cabin fever.

—7/15/80

I was not a happy man.

CHAPTER 9

W ITH THE EXCEPTION OF Saturday and Sunday we had been forced by the stormy seas to remain inside the house for a week and a half. The Chief, realizing we were losing a lot of overtime, put us to work in the main passageway, scraping and painting. It was a relief to get back to the mindless drudgery again.

Tony and I went to work sugieing the pump room. As it turned out, we had a great time. There is a therapeutic nature to cleaning things, and I got perverse pleasure from making the greasy walls and machinery glisten. Tony and I were becoming friends in the real sense of the word. His scolding the other day had been given in good faith. As Charlie said after he'd chewed out Spider, "That's what friends are for. You can yell at 'em and it won't make any difference."

Even Billy was in a better mood. He came into the pump room and sized up my work. "Looks good. Now that's the first thing you've done right." I could dig it, even though the son of a bitch wasn't giving me credit where credit was due.

Passing Diego Garcia gave us the opportunity to hear English-language radio for the first time in weeks. Being for the most part from Philly, most of the crew had been into boxing at one point or another. The overriding issue on the ship when we first tuned in to the army radio station that night was who won the Gerry Cooney–Sugar Ray Leonard fight. Our champion, the Bos, had it pretty much figured on Cooney. He'd met 'em all at one point or another: Joe Louis, Dempsey, and so on. It made him sick to see that the loser of the fight could clear a million.

"Jeez, back in the old days those guys'd fight for peanuts." Cooney won.

I saw a nebulous glowing (phosphorescent) blob float past us tonight. But earlier I was—while on the same evening watch—talking in dialogue to myself 'bout free will and the idealism of youth (where did it go, what was it, etc.) when I heard an uncanny and displaced cry, as if gulls of a singularly reptilian nature flew overhead. And in the afternoon I beheld a double rainbow so near you could almost touch it—but you can never grasp a rainbow. What should all about colors do!

—7/16/80

Ah, yes, ah, my . . .

—7/17/80

Well, today Tony informed me there was a flying fish on the portside, so I duly picked it up. The crew, to my somewhat startled amazement, was cheerfully enthusiastic, and Joe par-

ticularly encouraged me to stuff and mount it. Jake came up
with a plan for a board for it, and some shellac. It rained all
day today, and we stayed inside.

—7/18/80

They had been telling me about flying fish for some time now, but so far as I was concerned they were aerial myths. So it was with a mixture of doubt and excitement that I sneaked out onto the sea-washed deck to retrieve the lifeless carcass of the fish. The day before, Billy had been chosen to brave the storm and run out onto the deck to save the life preservers before they were swept overboard. It was actually a very scary moment; the ship was rolling more than the usual thirty degrees, and he had to make it back before the next wave crushed him against the bulkhead or washed him overboard. He rushed back into the house wet and bedraggled, asking, "Why weren't you watching for me?" We had been hanging out in the passageway. "That last one almost got me." As he spoke, a torrent of water crashed up against the house and shattered. Night or day, the ship's struggle against the ocean echoed through the house. At times the waves hit up to the third story. But today it was relatively peaceful, calm enough that we could venture out on deck between waves (which were hitting on a fairly regular basis, so that we could time it) but not so calm that we could stand outside for more than five minutes without getting our asses smashed against the cargo lines. In any event, I found the fish, a silver-blue thing not more than six inches long, floating in a pool that had collected on the deck. Poor bastard; it must have died an excruciating death: Its mouth was frozen by rigor mortis in an expression of horror, wide and gaping, a desperate attempt to get that last breath of air.

Miguel was the first to help. I'd brought it into the lounge, where the crew looked at it with interest. I hadn't a clue as to what to do with it, so Miguel took control. Waddling over to the kitchen sink, he washed it thoroughly. Then he whipped out one of the kitchen knives lodged in the butcher's block with an expert's finesse. It twirled in his hand like a butterfly. In one slick movement he slit open the belly and cleaned out the guts with his thumb. Rinsing the carcass out in a stream of cold water, he handed it to me before I knew it was done. I then understood he was a master chef.

I next took it up to my room, where I applied the taxidermy techniques I'd learned while working for the National Zoo. Having pinned the fish onto a piece of stiff cardboard, I stuffed it with a generous amount of cotton wool and placed it inside the chimney stack (it had two compartments that opened up), where the excessive heat of the great diesel engines below would dry it out.

Pleased with my handiwork, I returned to my duties. I had noted that according to the noon position we were fast approaching the equator, and I began an experiment in oceanographics. I proceeded directly to the toilet, which I shared with Eddie in the next room, grasped the handle firmly, and flushed. It was a success: The water drained out to the left. In a word: counterclockwise.

Well, this morning I saw twice the dusky white form of a bird flying. Also, part two of my scientific experiment: The

water by 4:30 this afternoon was spinning counterclockwise.
This fact is supported by the findings of a comparable inves-
tigation. Two weeks to go. I steered through a zero-visibility
storm today.

—7/19/80

That afternoon watch was quite something else. We'd been outside for two days now, but only on the stack deck; it was still too dangerous to go lower. And as anticipation of Japan increased, so too the crew got to speaking to one another. Out the window of the bridge I could barely see the ship rippling in the storm. Even a hulk as great as the *Rose City* buckled when lost in a fog-bound sea in the last throes of a typhoon.

It was my turn at the wheel when the storm got bad. They called Billy up for lookout even though it was still light out. For some reason the officers were drawn up to the bridge by the storm. I had long since switched to manual, and I silently kept to the course while they gathered about me. It was, to say the least, an interesting conflagration, er . . . constellation.

First mate, third mate, captain, me, second mate.

By now my ability to work the wheel was up to standard. That's another way of saying I could do it with the entire assembly of deck officers around me and not make a mistake. It was actually very simple once I got the hang of it. That wasn't much comfort, though. In two days we were going to reach the Straits of Malacca. As an ordinary, I was not permitted to steer while we were in the channel, but the others, except for Joe, were going to have to guide this time bomb through the treacherous waters off Malaysia and Indonesia, in this weather, without the help of radar. The Old Man was not going to listen to reason. We were going to do it, the Southeast Asian pirates armed with army-surplus grenade launchers and heat-seeking torpedoes be damned! There were orders, and that was that. Tough fucking luck if we cracked up on a sandbar; he was better paid than the whole lot of us.

There was an air of foreboding in the mess. It was as if we had all signed on for combat duty and the coming danger was pulling us all together. And if by chance we made it through the busiest sea channel in the world in typhoon season without radar in one piece, then to hell with the Old Man and his company. We'd be home free for "yang pussy." And liquor. And fresh food (our stores were running out).

Like the man said: "Terra Firma. The more firma, the less terra."

Saw some dark birds on the bow. Well, tomorrow we enter the Straits of Malacca, and bid adieu to the Indian Ocean. 'Twas rough all the way across, that's for sure. People keep saying how long it feels since we first got on; yes, I suppose it does . . . but this week spirits are good—I ain't been getting shit too much, and am in fact getting along . . .

—7/20/80

Today we entered the Straits of Malacca and saw both land and many vessels. But an extraordinary event took place in the morning lookout. I was on the starboard wing sitting on the bench, surveying casually the two-toned darkness of the sky

and sea. All of a sudden I looked out to my right (starboard)
and saw this big ol' fuckin' white bird sailing right up to me
1–2 yards away, the light having only just hit it then. Freaked,
I instantly ducked and promptly hit my head against the rail,
receiving a small quarter-inch cut on the bone between my eye
and my left temple. While the mate patched me up, the bird
swirled around overhead in the thick and muffled darkness.
Odd stuff, eh? So tonight I . . . received commissions from Joe
and Tony. The Bos found another flying fish, which I duly
stuffed. Used wire this time. We'll see.

—7/21/80

It was the first injury on the ship (the QMED's hernia not quali-
fying). Alone in the dark of morning lookout, I'd found myself
attacked by a seagoing dive-bomber, a vicious apparition of white
death bearing down on me. Dazed from my wound, I walked
through the bridge and into the bathroom to clean the blood off
my face. Billy noticed something was not quite right and came
over to see what was up. When the story came out, none of us
could help laughing, and tales of my adventure with the Killer
Sea Gull resounded through the passageways of the *Rose City.*

As for the flying fish, let's just say that my first endeavor was
not a failure by any means, but it did turn out looking like
a dried prune with wings. The drying in the stack deck took
about three days. I mounted it on a fresh piece of cardboard.
Then, when all was in readiness, I applied Jake's shellac, which
he had surreptitiously appropriated from the machine shop.
The result was a stiff, if not preserved, specimen of Exocoeti-
dae, suitable for framing.

The others were impressed with my handiwork and wanted a similar specimen for their own. Jake wanted one for his son, whom he talked about in mixed tones; Billy sought one for his three-year-old daughter. It hadn't occurred to them to save something so uniquely seaman-like as a flying fish for future posterity before. It was a novel idea, and they liked it.

With the second one I added some steel wool nabbed from the mess to keep the fish from shriveling up as the first had. I also monitored its progress in the stack more closely, since the arid conditions within had dried out the first specimen too much too soon.

In the lounge that morning Charlie figured out the expenses of running the ship. It took more than two million barrels of oil a year to power the *Rose City,* and they were slowing us down to 13 knots to "save energy." How many tankers did the company have out to sea? And how much did they really care about energy conservation if they were making their crews operate under such substandard conditions?

✳

When we entered the Straits of Malacca, on Monday, July 21, the weather was clear, and we were back on deck. At first there was a flurry of seagulls. Then the finches and sparrows appeared on deck. Before long the telltale wakes of other seagoing vessels ran in courses parallel to our own. We had reached civilization. There were sapient beings here, not just sea and sky.

We rounded the corner into the Straits sometime after noon. I'd been crashed out in my bunk when I woke up to a flurry of ships and islands. Unlike the smooth silhouettes of the South Sea Islands, these were rough-hewn. They shot straight up out of the water, and then mellowed into round, rolling jungle. It was as if a mason had smoothed off and planed away the circumference.

In the Straits were any number of small native craft. Some were junklike, others (steam) powered whalers. They nonchalantly passed us through the dirty water. There was more debris here than off the Cape: kitchen garbage, logs, even a single flip-flop. What had been the richest fishing grounds in the world only fifteen years earlier were now practically devoid of life.

On lookout that evening I watched the sun set over the hills of Malaysia. The good weather was still holding out, and it looked as though we were going to make it through the first of the three nights in the Straits all right. The Old Man was on the bridge that evening. The officers were trying not to show their concern, but they were obviously as worried about the lack of radar as we were. More so—they knew the full extent of the possible ramifications.

Through the twilight I spied two massive shadows coming toward us. The ship-to-ship radio crackled that they were a pair of U.S. Navy ships, a destroyer and an aircraft carrier, on their way to the Persian Gulf. Things had been heating up there; the Iranians and Iraqis were ready to go at it. That was not the best news we might have heard; there was a fifty-fifty chance we'd be assigned there after Japan.

The destroyer's "cutting edge" swept by us swiftly, its sleek dark outline barely visible against the twilight sky. Military ships did not have to display port and starboard lights—that would ruin the whole purpose of their cat-and-mouse game.

The carrier was somehow slower, like an avalanche when viewed from a distance; so gargantuan was its size that it appeared to be moving in slow motion. The Old Man sauntered out onto the wing to get a look at it as it passed us by. This was the one that had collided with the Panamanian tanker five days earlier. Crippled, it was on its way to Diego Garcia for repairs.

"They have worse crime rates on those ships than in most towns in America."

I looked at the Captain, amazed.

"Sure. They got over seven thousand men on those damn things. A guy gets paid off and he's rolled in the passageway before he can get back to his room. Christ, they got shopping malls, Burger Kings—the volunteer army gets all the low-lifes."

That blew me away. I stood there staring at this floating anthill for the next five minutes, its unbelievably complex labyrinth of high-tech conning towers and armaments hiding an entire city of troubadours. Shopping malls! Christ Almighty, we didn't even have a qualified medic.

The ship disappeared into the western night.

Today began—while I was washing windows—with my seeing a very curious creature, 'bout 1½ inches long, found on the bridge deck. I couldn't tell if it was a reptile, insect, animal, crustacean, or what! It crawled about, and as I tried to save it from the water of the hose (we were washing the windows) Jake said I'd better put it down—it might bite. Well, it might. Very curious.

—7/22/80

The Straits came and went. And during those three days it did not rain once. Three days in typhoon season, and it never rained. Everybody was relieved.

On watch, the Chief confided that there weren't even lighted buoys marking the channels. We'd been relying on the moonlight and the noon and horizon sun times. Those were the times the mates read the skies with their sextants. Each of them had a velvet-lined case for his personalized instrument. They'd strut out onto the wing at sunset, sunrise, and noon to take readings. It was partly tradition, partly security. A damn good thing it hadn't rained while we were in the Straits. No, scratch that—a miracle.

One night on watch, Tony told me, the Third mate came out onto the wing where my man was standing lookout. The Third was a cocky old-timer. Like Joe, he'd never bothered to advance his position. He didn't want to bother with all the added responsibilities; he liked it just where he was, thank you. Kind of a Walter Brennan character. Anyway, he came up to Tony with an officer-sized chip on his shoulder and started pointing out the stars. Tony had been to Kings Point Merchant Marine Academy, and this big lug, a nice enough fellow all the same, seemed at a loss as to the mysteries of the heavens.

Tony, ever polite, stood silently as the Third rambled on. After a point he had to intervene. If he was not mistaken, that constellation was Cassiopeia, not Orion. The Third stopped dead and looked at the able-bodied seaman. He turned around and disappeared behind the navigational partition of the bridge.

Tony waited. A few minutes later the Third reappeared. Behind the navigation partition were the books. In the books were the positions of the stars in every part of the known galaxy for every day of the year. By the Second's own admission, the mates never really bothered to read the stars; it was all there in the book. The Third had looked it up in the books.

The Third stared up at the night sky.

"I guess you're right."

He walked back onto the bridge and resumed his duties without ever saying another word to Able-Bodied-Seaman Holmes.

Tony and I had taken to talking to each other regularly on lookout. When he told me that story, he was delighted. He also dug having a confidant, and our rapport grew stronger with the lengthening days. While the rest of the crew suffered the slings and arrows of outrageous sobriety, Tony was fully laden with a stock of wine and Blue Ribbon. After a morning's OT, he'd slip me a beer in the understanding I'd tell no one. No problem.

When he'd come up to relieve me on lookout, I often found myself hanging out with him for upward of an hour. He'd read all the horror stories and delighted in relating them to someone. It was ghost tales around the campfire all over again. He also delighted in swallowing the red-hot stub of his cigar.

We sailed out of the Straits into the South China Sea. Rounding the corner at Singapore Island, we were suddenly cut off by a Greek lumber ship. It came within twenty yards of us, cruising through the waves like a drunk Indian in a Trans Am. At dinner Charlie started bitching about the incompetence of foreign-flag ships, the flag-of-convenience vessels that American companies were now using to cut down costs (and subsequently killing the Merchant Marine, which was a pitiful twenty percent of what it was in World War II, when the Merchants suffered more casualties than all other branches of the military combined, as they'd been doing convoy duty for three years before we actually entered the war). They were for the most part Liberian. Then Greek. Then Panamanian. The governments didn't ask any questions, and there weren't any safety standards to worry about.

Charlie took command of the dinner conversation.

"Those no-good motherfuckers. I was going to moon them when I remembered they were Greek."

There was general laughter. Then I dredged up a joke from the bottom of the barrel.

"How do you separate the men from the boys in Greece?"

The crew didn't know.

"With a crowbar."

They broke out into long and loud peals of laughter. The gag had worked.

The waiting had become overwhelming. We were off the Gulf of Thailand with only about a week to go, but the time was passing incredibly slowly. We watched the same movies over and over again. By now we'd seen *High Plains Drifter* twenty times and knew every line in the film. There was a magnificent grace to Clint's performance. With a minimum of words he carried one of the great Westerns of all time. None of us grew tired of it, either. He was too cool, too Clint. The three Woody Allen movies on the ship, however, were complete bombs. Only *Love and Death,* which Bud liked, was shown more than once. These guys wanted guts, not neuroses.

That night Joe told me about the "green flash." When it's perfectly clear in the equatorial zone a brilliant green flash illuminates the sky just as the sun goes down over the horizon. Unfortunately, there were always a few too many clouds around for me to see it, and it happens only under certain specific meteorological conditions.

Overtime now took place out in the blistering tropical heat. The sun beat down on the steel deck and roasted us like spring chickens. Everyone moved slowly, sluggishly, resisting the temptation to collapse where he stood. The Chief put me to work banging out the rust on the deck with a nine-pound hammer. When he'd pass me by, Tony'd break into a refrain of "John Henry."

It was satisfying work. Billy called me "Ahab the Arab," for the white rag I'd wrapped around my head in Berber fashion as I worked, squatting like an Indian, swinging the hammer up and letting it fall with a bang. The others moved in a similar rhythm, the scrapers and brushes grinding languidly in the equatorial heat.

On the night of the twenty-fifth we passed our sister ship, the *Beaver State* (i.e., Oregon, whose capital is the so-called Rose City of Portland), on its way to Sumatra from Japan. This was bad news, since we were probably bound for the Persian Gulf now that the *Beaver State* was taking our planned route. On the previous trip, *Rose City* was stuck for a month off Kuwait, and the crew was allowed ashore once. Not that it mattered; there was no drinking in the port, and no women. Spirits sank.

"those are my favorite subjects: gravity & weight"
—Tessa 11/30/89

This was the longest single stretch at sea any of the crew had taken, with one or two exceptions. Now it looked as though we were going to have to do it all over again after a day or two in Japan.

Well, five daze to go. So tonight we had a "Funky Union Meeting," as Tony described it. The Bos would call upon the various department delegates (Jake—Deck, Miguel—Steward, Frank—Engine), then the treasurer (the steward), and then go through the various items, routinely asking if there was any discussion therein and saying, "What's your pleasure?" and then going on to the next item without waiting for a response. Jake put up a couple of resolutions, both unanimously passed. The first called for transportation money back home from both foreign and domestic trips. The second was to make any bosuns or delegates who failed to report C and B cards when entering a home port donate $50 to SPAD (the political branch of the union). He was getting more and more worked up about it. Later he and Tony (to whom the resolution was largely directed) had a heated discussion. There were also citations against the lack of a payroll, and against Sparks for his neglect on the flower front (he was supposed to have wired flowers to the wives of several of the crew, a tradition in the Merchants, but claimed he couldn't find a shop that would do it; as Billy said, "All Radio Operators are Bed Bugs"). The Bosun said, "We will now stand a solemn minute for departed brothers," and everyone suddenly rose and stood in a pleasing, respectful silence.

—7/27/80

And time slowly passed. I heard "Funky Town" in Chinese while passing Taiwan, and Jake gave Jimmy and me a lesson in splicing wire cable. Jake had gotten very vocal on the matter of union politics. He went into wild harangues about the corruption of a once great union. The SIU had fought the Teamsters in the sixties, and beat them. The Philly hall had a semitruck driven through it, and several brothers were worked over or shot. But the SIU had won, and Jimmy Hoffa was discredited. For Jake these glory days had long since passed, and it infuriated him. He'd talk till his blood pressure rose like the stock market on a killer day.

I listened, but nobody else did. They'd heard it all before. And they'd also seen Jake at the big meetings in Philly: silent and doting like one of the sheep. Dave Martin had made his stand a few times before the union bosses, but he never had the support of the brothers. It was too much to ask of them to face their leaders; it was too easy to follow the crowd. Out at sea it might be a different story, brothers full of anger and new ideas, but on the beach it was a cat-and-mouse game as to who would get the next of the very few jobs. To tick off the bosses was to write yourself out of the market. To follow their orders was to keep working.

We passed the island of Luzon, the main island of the Philippines, during the full moon. The water was like liquid emerald coated with mother-of-pearl and sparkling fish scales.

On the twenty-ninth we picked up Japanese TV. It was great. It didn't matter that we couldn't understand a word—it was something new, something different. On a talk show they followed the American patterns, but bowed to one another every thirty seconds, never quite giving up their old ways.

Flies began to appear on deck; we were getting close. I was sitting in my room when Tony banged on my door and said he'd seen some flying fish in the water. He'd never seen them before, and he was very excited. They darted 150 feet above the water, flapping their wings like hummingbirds.

On overtime we were painting the deck itself. The hot work on the bow was often accompanied by the tension generated by the mates watching from the bridge. In the last few weeks they had particularly taken to watching us, gathering around in groups as big as three or four. The crew was increasingly annoyed by this. Once, when Tony painted JOHN SUCKS on the deck as he worked to give me a hard time as I watched from up on the bridge, the Chief came over and looked down at him. I figured Tony was probably bummed he'd been seen goofing off, but when I saw him later, he said, "Good! Fuck him!"

That was becoming the general attitude: "Fuck 'em!"

On watch that night a voice came over the ship-to-ship radio: "To all ships. This is a Russian destroyer. Get out of our way. We are coming through. We repeat: Get out of our way." The etiquette of the sea did not concern them. Come too close and you are in trouble.

The next morning I got my first look at flying fish in action. They were great. They zigzagged over the waves like bees. It was their way of avoiding the jaws of a "natural selector."

Later in the day I was reprimanded for walking barefoot through the corridors: "If you cut yourself there's no way you'll have a case." It wasn't concern for my personal safety that spurred them on; they were just trying to teach me the way of the sea.

The tension has been building up for daze. The mate and the Bosun have both been bird-dogging us while on deck. Billy has yelled up at the bridge in anger (though no one was there). Then yesterday at lunch Joe was asking the Bos about why the mate was bird-dogging us, and the Bos got all excited, yelling: "You ain't on the fucking deck. If he was out there I'd tell him!"

Said Joe: "I can see through the fucking port hole!" etc.

Tension.

Now there is the question of breaking sea watch while in port. Billy started, I believe, the rumor that the mate would let us vote on it. He and Bud were originally adamant that we should break watch, while Jake would preach for hours that we shouldn't. But one day (yesterday) in the hot fucking sun chipping and scraping with the bird-dogs (the Bos included) convinced everyone that we shouldn't break watch.

"I'm liable to lose seven hours of overtime a day," said Jake, exasperated, and so on.

Well, today I go up to the bridge. The mate (I had the second wheel) says: "That Jake is too much."

I say, "How so?"

The mate says, "He comes up to me and asks, 'Well, Mate, what's it going to be? A vote on the sea watches?'" The mate giggles. "Hmph! Fuck that shit, no one ever heard of voting on sea watches. That fucking guy has been out here thirty-five years . . ."

I play along with him, as I'm trying to be as neutral as possible.

"What is this? A pleasure cruise?" he continues. "If we stay more than two weeks we'll break watches for sure . . ." Etc.

At breakfast, at my usual table with the Bos and Peanuts, I relay the news that there is no vote. The Bos gets pissed.

8:00 a.m.—ALL HANDS—breaking out lines. As the whole crew works, the mate shows up and starts talking to the Bos, who's at the winch.

BOS: *I hear you might break sea watches, Mate.*

MATE: *If we're in the port more than a couple of days, yes. (he looks away)*

BOS: *Then you're going to have some fucking trouble! (his voice rises)*

MATE: *What the hell are you talking about? We can't just keep paying these guys . . .*

(The conversation turns into an argument.)

BOS: *Look, if someone hits me in the fucking balls I'm going to hit right back! (referring to our loss of overtime) We'll go right to the fucking captain!*

MATE: *Look! I run the fucking deck department!*

BOS: *I don't give a fuck! We get screwed while everybody else gets overtime! We'll stop right now.*

MATE: *Fuck you! (He is adamant now, but clearly nervous because he has no control, and people are watching now. The Bos starts yelling, making like he's ready to pop the mate.)*

BOS: *Now you leave my men alone; we don't want you spooking them on deck.*

MATE: *Fuck you! You can't just tell me what to do . . .*

(The Bos turns off the winch. Work stops. Jake and Billy firmly sit down as the Bos signals. All the others drop the lines except Bud, who keeps trying to work.)

BOS: *I don't give a fuck. Let's just get this shit over with.*

(Everyone else stands up and goes over to the rail, where they await the Bos's signal. The mate stares down at the Bos, dumbfounded. The Bos stares back up at the mate with his great arms loose and ready at his sides. After a minute's silence the mate turns and walks off, uttering a string of obscenities. The crew cheers and work resumes.)

BOS: *We got a fucking union on here! We got a crew of Philly Sea Lawyers!*

—7/31/80

Channel fever—we all had it. One more day and we'd be off this stinking tub after seven weeks at sea. I read the Tarot and came up with the cards for Strength, Friendship, Opportunity, and Misguided Motivations. The final outcome was the Five of Pentacles: Obtuseness.

The food had gotten downright terrible. Provisions were so low that Miguel was scraping the bottom of every barrel for each meal. The thought of some tasty Kobe beef lingered in our minds.

As if to make up for this, the steward calmly strutted into the lounge that last morning at sea and sat himself down in the central chair.

"Now hear this," he began, his deep, throaty voice capturing the startled attentions of the collected company. He wasn't looking at anybody in particular; he was looking at a convention that he'd been asked to call to order. "The orders have come in. We are going to be in Japan for three weeks."

The crew broke out into cheers. It was just what the doctor ordered—rest, relaxation, and any number of wild nights ashore. My prospects for Japan were somewhat less colorful than the others'. I'd been there twice before, and had been a student of Japanese culture for a number of years. To me this trip afforded an invaluable opportunity to visit the cities of Nara and Kyoto, to see firsthand and on my own time the peculiarities of this strange island.

To the crew the trip offered an opportunity to get insanely intoxicated, to experience the peculiarities of the inscrutable geisha girls. The Bosun's running joke was that "The Japanese pussy runs east-west," said as he carved a horizontal line in the air before him. The old-timers had been to Japan any number of times before, some of them right after the war, when snipers would take shots at Americans from the hills. They had seen it when a dollar satisfied the whores and rickshaws were the only way to travel.

Now they bitched at how expensive it was, and how the Japanese no longer had any respect for Americans and their dollar bills. Even so, it was good to be in the Far East. These were seamen who preferred Asia to Europe. There was more action, more fun, and more for your money. When we were passing the Philippines, the Bosun pointed in the direction of Manila and with a pained, longing look in his eyes said it was "the best liberty port in the whole fucking world."

In the passageway between the mess and the lounge Jake and some of the others had posted a couple of arrival pools. For ten bucks a shot you could pick the part of the hour when the ship would drop anchor. The minutes were actually hidden, so your choice was completely random. This gave rise to great speculation. Tony and I went in together on three or four numbers, with the agreement that we'd split the winnings. Miguel was by far the most eager bettor, spending almost as much as was in the pot. He didn't care; he lived for cheap thrills.

Peanuts was a veteran of the arrival-pool circuit. When he used to work on passenger ships he'd rake in buckets of cash from unwitting passengers. Drawing up a secret-ballot sign-up sheet, he'd carefully note where the quarter-hour lots had "randomly" been placed and give those to his buddies. Then he'd pass the sheet around to the guests. The reason for this was quite simple: On passenger ships they logged the official time of arrival to the nearest quarter of an hour. Thus Peanuts, taking his percentage, won every time.

The day inched forward. On watch, the Chief was very subdued. He shuffled about the bridge in a sulky silence. He had definitely lost the battle with the crew and lost face with everyone on the ship. It was most satisfying.

When watch was finally over it was time to let loose. I'd carefully saved three beers for Jake, Billy, and me for this last night and now broke them out. Jake took his almost for granted, walking off with Joe and drinking it immediately. Billy was actually touched. He was also already drunk; earlier in the day Tony had relented and sold him and Ned a case of Blue Ribbon. (There was nothing to lose; he could stock up again in Japan.) The two of them immediately set about drinking it, and were smashed by eight p.m. I had the last wheel watch, so I didn't make it down to give Billy his beer until then. When I saw that I was a bit late, I was slightly disappointed, but I gave it to him anyway. Reeling through the halls, he showed everybody what his watch partner had done.

Other crew members were also drunk on Tony's booze. Peanuts, Tony's watch partner, gulped down a bottle of vodka. It made him crazy—he had that manic look in his eye street tramps get when they get the "horribles." He weaved back and forth, staring in icy silence into your subconscious through his bloody pupils, and then shouted some insult or hellish oath against you.

I sat for the most part in the darkened lounge watching a bizarre Japanese soap opera about World War II and drinking my last beer. Then Tony came in with a three-foot bottle of Italian chianti he'd been saving and poured me a huge glass. Delicious. I took to calling him a great man, and, after a few more drinks, a genius.

When the time came to hit the sack I made my way upstairs via the outside route. On gaining the stack, I came across Billy, Ned, Charlie, and the boys, all smashed and lying on lounge chairs they'd brought out to the deck. Ned called me over. They were all in a great mood and slapped me on the back. Hell, it was over; it was all downhill from here.

Then Ned got all bug-eyed. "Did you have a number?"

I'd forgotten all about the pot. After my exchange with Spider, I'd mentioned it to no one on the ship. Then Billy and Charlie had started talking about the Angolan reefer one morning and I freaked. As it turned out, Billy was the one who had sold Spider the pot in the first place. That was a load off my mind—at least we now had some common ground.

That was a few weeks after we'd left Angola, and in the following weeks Pete, the cadet, and Charlie would bum a joint or two off me now and then; it was a good ice-breaker. But this was the first time Ned, my confirmed adversary, had ever mentioned it to me. In fact, this was about the first conversation we'd ever had that wasn't tinged with suspicion and hate. Unfortunately I'd stashed the weed in the forepeak for the customs inspection, and there was no way to go out there now without the mates on the bridge getting suspicious. Nonetheless, it had somehow brought me into the realm of being one of the boys. Things were lightening up and cooling.

Part II

SEA STORIES

CHAPTER 10

AUGUST 1, 1980. Osaka Harbor. We pulled into Kii-suido Bay in the silver twilight before the dawn. I walked out to the foredeck with the Bosun and helped him drop anchor. There was so much traffic in and out of Osaka Harbor (which also serviced Sakai and Kove) that there was a waiting list for pilots. We waited in the cool air, surrounded by the velvet islands that defined the bay. Overhead an origami flock of snow geese flew by.

Miguel had won the pool and cleaned up a cool two hundred. He immediately began planning how he was going to spend it. Jumping up and down, he made specific gestures and references to various aspects of the female anatomy.

Dead tired from the previous night's celebration, I went back to bed as soon as possible. When I woke and stumbled out onto deck we were moving again, through green, rocky islands. It was bright and sunny.

I met up with Billy in front of the house. He was in a quiet, comfortable mood. We leaned over the rail and enjoyed the cooling breeze and the warming sun. He told me that customs had already cleared the ship and that mail was waiting for us at the other end. Every now and then you could see a hidden temple nestled into the face of one of the passing islands.

Osaka Harbor was a great parking lot. There were an estimated thirty ships at anchor, all waiting to dock. Producing only one percent of the oil they consumed, the Japanese were hoarding. Our three-week wait was the result of overbooking—they had nowhere to put our load. The shoreline was the basic refuse of the industrial society: refineries, factories, toxic-waste dumps, warehouses. Off on the eastern shore, looking down on the smog-covered chrome complexes, a long pagoda stood out in a small patch of green.

There was one drawback to our victory over the Chief: Since we were still working the daily sea watches, there wasn't time to go ashore. The cards were now in the officers' hands. After a series of negotiations it was decided we could share watches on a rotating basis. That would give us every other day ashore. In addition, there was a proviso in our contract that we got one day off for every sixty days of work. You take what you can get.

Only Joe and the chief engineer were able to get ashore the first night. The chief engineer was a good man; he'd started as an ordinary and worked his way through the ranks. Hanging out with him was not like being with an officer.

The rest of us sat up and watched the shore. In the distance was a tremendous display of fireworks, as if they knew we'd arrived. It was frustrating being stuck out in the bay, but not nearly as bad as being out at sea. The television kept our attention, and the sparkle of the city lights kept our imagination. The old-timers were somewhat indifferent. They still talked about going ashore and finding the nearest whorehouse, but we knew they wouldn't. They were too old and tired for that. Most of them would find a friendly bar and stay there until they had drunk themselves silly. The Bosun would go have a good meal, after having called home first; his condition forbade drinking. What we'd heard about in their sea stories were the antics of the boys now. Billy, Ned, Charlie, Bud, Jimmy, and me. That was something they really wanted to see—me going out on the town. I think they thought I was still a virgin.

The night passed and morning came. Gangway watch had gone into effect, so only one of us had to go on top of it at a time. Being on top of it meant sitting out by the gangway in case a boat came up alongside. Joe and the engineer had returned the same night in a foul mood. We were officially registered in Sakai, a small town outside of Osaka. This entailed a forty-minute launch ride from the ship to the docks. To make matters worse, when the two of them finally got into the town, it was after hours.

"Can you believe that? The no-good motherfuckin' Nips didn't want anything to do with us. Wouldn't take our fuckin' money. I tell you, this is a shit port! A shit port!" Joe was enraged, especially about the money. I pointed out to him that if a Jap walked into a bar in South Philly and handed the waiter a yen note he'd be thrown out, to which he replied, "Yeah, but this is different."

On the next afternoon watch it was my turn to sit by the gangway first. Tony joined me, as he was getting ready to go ashore on the next launch. We'd been going over the things we wanted to do in Japan and had agreed that the single outstanding attraction was the shopping centers. Huge complexes of futuristic buildings spread out for miles in the heart of every self-respecting Japanese metropolis. They were electronic playgrounds where you could lose yourself for hours.

Waiting there also gave us a chance to go over the first half of the voyage. We had made it without radar; navigated safely through the Straits on the three nights of the rainy season when it didn't rain; burned forward when the tanks were light; and chipped and scraped in the presence of highly volatile fumes. Thinking on all this took our breath away—it was the first time we'd realized what a maniac the Old Man was. Pete, whose duty it was to clean the officers' bathrooms and make up their bunks, said the Captain slept with all his clothes on, on top of the blankets. Once Ned was ordered to wake the Old Man and found him sitting in his room with the curtains and shades drawn tight, his sunglasses on, smoking his cigar.

The cigar reminded Tony of one of his new pastimes. The Old Man had run out of the brand of cigars he liked to smoke and was reduced to buying the heinous stogies in the ship's store. They smelled horrible, and not a one was properly rolled. Tony, on the other hand, had a generous stock of fine tobacco products. In addition to his custom-blended pipe tobacco, he enjoyed a variety of Cuban and other quality cigars. On learning that the Old Man had run out, Tony took to taking a cigar with him to the bridge and slowly lighting it up, savoring every puff. One day, not being able to control himself any longer, the Old Man remarked on what a fine aroma Tony's cigar exuded. Tony turned to the Old Man and said, yes, in fact it was an excellent cigar, and with his disarming smile returned to his duties, never once offering the Captain one.

There were other signs of the new tension between the officers and the crew. "Why they're breaking out with this shit now, after a good voyage, is a mystery," Tony said to me. It was true that the trip, an excessively long one, had no fights or outstanding arguments among the crew—something of a record. But now the officers had taken to busting our asses, letting on that they thought we were incompetent knaves. The stoppage of work when coming into the bay was the final straw, so far as they were concerned. What was once a bunch of badly paid idiots was now a threat to the officers' absolute authority.

Tony, Ned, and some of the others went ashore that night. God only knew when I'd get a chance. Then Billy spoke up to the Bosun, complaining that the 4–8 watch was getting the shaft and wanted to split tomorrow. It was done, and Billy and I agreed to leave together on the first launch after the morning watch and meet up with Ned on the docks. Our time had finally come.

The shuttle ride took forever. It was a small launch that went around to the various tankers and relayed the crews from ship to shore. Billy and I were antsy as hell.

Joe and Jake pointed out the various ships in the harbor. In drydock were Indian frigates, coal ships, and great huge cranes and construction harnesses used to overhaul their rusting hulls. In a shower of sparks the white-suited technicians ran around, inspecting the work. On the quay below, ragged fishermen sat patiently waiting for a bite from whatever fish might still be living in these incredibly polluted waters.

We finally reached the shore. On the dock the steward and

MAY 19 1581990-7 1   08/19/80

MOYNIHAN
#142 RUSSELL SENATE OFF BLDG
WASHINGTON DC 20510

AIL
REO

3'

HIYA FOLK!

Well its almost 8 weeks since we left Eagles Point, and we are currently on the hook (at anchor for all you land lubbers out there) in Osaka bays. We've been told we were going to be here for two weeks, and while many of the crew Members construed in their favor the positives complaining. I can see certain advantages to being in Japan we might be here for as much as a month coming back sometime in October thus a semester off has been predetermined by APEX MARINE.

Well the trip from Angola to Japan was a busy one, 5 weeks, But I really, as we dive get ashore in Angola, the crew is apparently an exceptional one as my fellows Remark with relief & surprise we had NO Beefs nor fights, and everyone handled the intense excitement well. For me it was a great novelty to see Cape Town off the coasts of Mallorca, Phillipines and Sumatra. I also saw some South Sea islands, and believe it or not here is what they look like:

I always thought they were w.ld.ng.
I also saw my first flying fish
which don't about the water like a french, actually flying, and so when one is found in a grim state of rigor mortis

Ned awaited the launch. I rushed up the boardwalk and kissed the ground. The steward laughed at me and got on the launch to return to the ship. We helped Ned put his stores on the launch (his stores consisting of two gallons of vodka, two gallons of gin, a fifth of rum, and a case of beer) and, along with Sparks, who was not required to do anything while we were in port, we grabbed a taxi and took off for Osaka.

The first woman I had seen was fishing by the pier, but I hardly noticed her. Now, caught in the traffic jams of the city, I saw a menagerie of gorgeous, cosmopolitan ladies. We were freaking out. One woman, in the car next to us, waved and smiled to us. It was almost too much.

Osaka seemed unreal: Vast avenues lined with neon-covered skyscrapers. Sidewalks packed with bustling Japanese. Stores. Bars. Restaurants. Automobiles.

We got out at Osaka Station, roughly the center of town, and set about the first order of business: getting a drink. Ned had been stationed in Yokohama and had a working vocabulary of Japanese. He could swear (always the first priority), bargain, and ask where the nearest gin mill was. Alas, luck was not with us that day, and we wandered through the backstreets for half an hour before we found a place where they served liquor. But it was worth it.

It was our first drink ashore after fifty-three days. Billy held the glass up to the light and contemplated it with a connoisseur's expertise. The managers were very friendly and watched us with curiosity. Our waiter was dressed in a special maître d's jacket and had obviously been sent over due to his understanding of English. Our moans of delight were, however, untranslatable. From the kitchen door a fat woman giggled at us.

Having satiated our initial desire, we struck out again. It was curious—the only parts of town that seemed remotely Asian were the back alleys. The main streets were all modern, the people all dressed like Madison Avenue executives or Greenwich Village hipsters. I saw two women in kimonos and they looked uncomfortably out of place. As if in empathy, a strange old man, squatting in a dirty backstreet shack, laughed at me knowingly.

Wandering around in amazement, we stumbled onto the amusement district, a network of covered alleys that stretched endlessly in every direction. Hawkers in front of every store clapped their hands and shouted at every passerby to come in. Electronic games, the likes of which are only now invading this country, rang out deafeningly. Groovy young couples bopped their way through the crowds, wearing what we later came to know as Sony Walkmans, but none of us had ever seen them before. Gaudy nightclubs played loud music and promised wild times. That rang a bell in Billy's and Ned's ears, but none would be open until later that night.

Whores. Lots of them, and right now! That's all the two of them could think about. Sparks and I tried to hide our mutual nervousness—he because he was a middle-aged square, and I because I'd never been to a cathouse. We found one club that looked promising, The Pink Lady. An awkward rendering of a naked lady surrounded by flashing lights bespoke geisha girls and hot sake. The four of us climbed down the stairs into an empty bar and dead silence. The proprietor came out and asked us what we would like. Then in the back room someone turned on the strobe lights and disco music. We took a look around and decided to get the hell out of there.

Ned then wanted to find a *bar*. But we found no satisfaction—only restaurants that served beer. Begrudgingly he accepted the inevitable, and we entered the next one we came across. It was clearly a higher-class joint than we'd anticipated. The décor was traditional Japanese elegant, and the customers were well dressed. No matter; they had drink, and we had money. Lots of it.

After three or four rounds of pint-sized bottles of Asahi beer the atmosphere was relaxed. With every gulp there was a toast, and with every toast we got louder. Billy raised his glass and slapped me on the knee.

"Can you believe this goofy motherfucker is a senator's son?"

Things were all right, and the dog days were over.

Soon we were back on the street, reeling and swaying through crowds of shoppers. I had stopped to pick up a poster for a professional wrestling match as a souvenir for a friend of mine when I noticed that a thin, distinguished gentleman in a gray flannel suit was tailing us. The reason I knew this was that I had seen him in three different places around the bazaar. I passed the word on to my comrades, and we proceeded to try to ditch him. No dice—he was a cop, and he had us pegged. Then again, we weren't hard to find. I alone was a foot taller than anyone for miles, and we weren't the quietest bunch, either.

A regular policeman with a walkie-talkie stopped us and waited for the plainclothesman to show up, which he promptly did. What were we up to, and where were we from? It didn't seem exactly fair; we hadn't broken anything or been outrageous in our conduct.

Looking back on it, I think it was the pursuit of the whores that brought us to his attention. Billy and Ned had been stopping people and asking about ladies, using sign language to illustrate their desires. That was taboo; the Japanese tend to clothe their emotions in blankets of serenity and discuss them only behind closed . . . screens?

The cop just wanted to make contact and let us know he was on to us. We weren't detained from our wanderings for more than a few minutes. Slightly enraged, Billy and Ned were now in a feisty mood, and more than ever ready for a good time.

Continuing down the street, we came across a gambling joint. It was too much. Slot machines, blackjack, roulette. Sparks and I jumped to it, cashing in our yen for tokens and pouring them into the slot machines. Billy and Ned weren't quite so enthusiastic. They watched us for a while, throwing away an occasional yen. A Japanese fellow who'd been hanging out in the place struck up a conversation with them. They were both trashed and were laughing at everything he said. The fellow picked up on it and began laughing too. But soon the novelty wore off and Billy and Ned said they were going to a bar the man had told them about and would meet us back in the gaming hall in a few minutes.

Sparks and I kept playing. On the machine next to mine a fellow was raking in jackpot after jackpot. It was incredible. I asked him his secret, to which he replied in Pidgin English that it was the number of coins you put in that gave you the best odds. I followed his example and hit the jackpot myself. Delighted with my luck, I went up to the cashier to turn in my tokens. She looked at me and smiled, pointing to the multilingual sign that hid in the darkest corner of the room:

GAMES ARE FOR ENJOYMENT ONLY. NO MONEY WILL BE GIVEN
OUT.

Disgusted, I walked away with Sparks and handed my mentor all the tokens I'd won. Strange people, strange people . . .

Billy and Ned, as was to be expected, did not return. Sparks
was a square, and I wasn't up for what they wanted, so they
blew us off. No problem—we actually felt like taking it easy,
anyway. We strolled into a shopping mall and picked up some
maps of the town. On my recommendation Sparks bought a
copy of *The Tale of Genji*.

Having done this, we stepped into a backstreet noodle joint
for dinner. The beer flowed and the noodles were fine. At that
point anything tasted better than what we'd been getting on
the ship.

There is a strange cult in this world not known to the population at large. It is less flamboyant than the International Society of Odd Fellows, and more mysterious than the Knights of
Columbus. Its ways make the Masons look like novices. This
cult is that of the Golden Horde, a select group of people who
realize and edify the glory of Genghis Khan. As it happened,
both Sparks and I were active members.

Sparks was a very intelligent man. He'd worked for the military in the Arctic Circle, on the DEW line, and had joined the
Merchant Marine as the result of what appeared to have been
a midlife crisis. It was a joy for me to find another as worked
up as I was about the Mighty Khan, the great unsung genius.

But the time had come to return to the ship, and after navi-
gating our way via the railroad to Sakai (which involved nu-
merous wrong stops, stilted conversations with policemen, and
various taxi rides), we awaited the launch on the dock.

The launch went out only every four hours, and if Billy and Ned were going to make watch they had to catch this midnight ride. But they never showed up. Sparks and I were wondering what to do when a nervous Japanese businessman showed up. He was a company representative, and he told us they were in jail.

CHAPTER 11

THE OLD-TIMERS TOOK the news with an air of "I told you so!" smugness. Billy and Ned were troublemakers! What the fuck did they think they were doing? Who the fuck did they think they were? Etc., etc. . . .

Charlie and I smiled at each other when we heard them bitching. He leaned over to me and said, "Those motherfuckers—they pulled the same exact fucking shit in their day, and now look at them, cackling like a bunch of old ladies."

The old-timers were now generally to be found in the mess, while the boys hung out in the lounge. It was the beginning of the second distinction on the ship: officers vs. men; old-timers vs. the boys. Not that the latter conflict bred much ill will. It was mostly a question of the old-timers wanting to sleep at night and the boys being sick of hearing the same stories from World War II over and over again.

Our two war heroes returned to duty that afternoon. They'd been fined and let out on their own recognizance. That was generally the practice with seamen or sailors in any port; it was to be expected.

In a party held in Jimmy's room that night the true story

came to light. Ned and Billy had wandered off to a bar and gotten trashed. Ned fell asleep at the bar, and Billy was in a state of complete incoherence. He managed to get up and go to the bathroom at one point, but while he was in there a cop burst in and grabbed him from behind. Billy wheeled around and KO'd the cop, then ran out to get Ned. Mama-san had called the cops while Billy was in the bathroom, and the thin man who'd been following us was right there. It seems when we split up he'd felt it wise to follow those two. Billy didn't get very far before the riot police were on him. It wouldn't have been so bad if he'd stuck to his fists. Unfortunately, Billy bit a policeman in the chest, apparently ripping out a fair-sized chunk of his flesh, and that's when the nightsticks fell.

So far as the boys were concerned, they were heroes. The liquor flowed and the jokes got worse but somehow funnier. Billy came up to me and shook my hand, saying, "You goofy motherfucker!" Then he put on a concerned, innocent tone: "What happened to you guys? Ned and I went to a bar, had one drink, and that was it." He felt guilty for ditching us, but it was no problem—we were getting along and it was all right.

The party continued. Billy turned to me an hour later and said, with less guilt this time, "How'd it go with you guys? We missed you; did you wait there? We showed up. But, hey, a good fuckin' time, huh? Yeah, a GOOD FUCKING TIME!!"

The boys began to notice that Billy was getting particularly drunk. He was swaying about the room with his drink and shouting every word. We had all tried to phone home in Osaka, but none of us had gotten through. That hurt Billy especially. He and his wife were not getting along at all when he left, and it had been eating away at him for two months now.

Where was she? Why wasn't there anyone at home? Worse yet, when he tried again, a recording came on and said the number had been changed.

The third time Billy turned to me he was mad. "Where were you guys? We waited for you but you never showed up!"

Then Billy snapped. I'd seen it before with a friend of mine who'd taken acid and didn't know how to handle it. The subconscious took over; he wasn't the same person. No one in the room was the same to him, and nothing that had gone on over the last two months was as it had been. Like a prophet, he went around to each of us, one by one. Each person in the room received a full analysis of himself from deep down inside the man's primal fears.

Jimmy and the cadet were noticeably shaken. Ned had passed out, so there was no one to help Billy. He was lost, completely lost. Charlie tried to carry the conversation as if nothing was wrong, but Billy's ravings silenced him.

After this had gone on for half an hour, the cadet took to talking about it to his face. Billy couldn't hear; he was lost.

"Gee, I'd like to do something for the guy, but what the fuck," the cadet said.

I signaled to the cadet to stop it. I was trying to talk him down, but it wasn't working. He was too far gone, and I was still a newcomer. Billy just kept it up, preaching to his captive audience until we finally made excuses and went off to bed.

Billy was not the only one who'd undergone a personality change. While his was an extreme example, Bud, Peanuts, and many of the others were very different now that they had booze whenever they wanted. Which was all the time.

The next morning, life went on without further mention of the incident with Billy. Bud stayed on after his watch and stuck around in the lounge. He was overwhelmingly relieved to have a good stiff drink again. He offered me a scotch and I accepted. Despite his uncannily good mood, however, he was still apt to bitch.

"This trip has been a fucking disaster," he said. He wasn't in his element. He was too physically perfect, too noble in his manner. As it turned out, he was a college dropout and came from a family that lived in a wealthy suburb of Wilmington. But he was also a surly malcontent, and had taken to the sea with a vengeance.

This morning his main entertainment was a Japanese porno magazine that he had picked up in Sakai. The law in Japan was somewhat arbitrary—you could buy pornography in vending machines anywhere around the city, but the pornography could not show any sexual organs other than the woman's breasts. Thus one often found the standard centerfold crudely defaced by the publisher, who had scratched out the genitalia with a knife. In the high-class magazines, such as the Japanese *Playboy*, an airbrush was used to smooth out any offensive material.

CHAPTER 12

A T FIRST I THOUGHT it was my imagination, a projection of my pirate fantasies. I could have sworn I'd seen well over a dozen people that first day ashore wearing eye patches. The second venture into Osaka confirmed this. Yes, there was in fact an inordinate number of people with cumbersome gauze bandages over their eyes.

I figured it had something to do with the terrible Japanese pollution. We had all heard the horror stories about schoolchildren wearing gas masks, and about the fresh-air vending machines. I was mistaken, however. The oil company had sent a watchman to the ship while we were in the harbor, a nice fellow who spoke good English and gave us tips on the town. When I asked him about the eye patches he explained that they were from plastic surgery. In Japan big Western eyes had become very chic, and hundreds of Japanese were having operations on their eyes, widening them, one at a time.

Our friend the watchman lived in one of the empty cabins on B deck. When he wasn't talking to the chief about port logistics (which was very seldom) he could be found in the lounge, watching TV with the crew.

I still hadn't called home, though, and for my second foray I asked the watchman to write down the location of some place where I could call the States. He was glad to do this, and on the back of the map he'd given me he scrawled the address in Japanese. Underneath he wrote the English translation: THE GLAND HOTEL.

It wasn't long before we were all accustomed to the new way of life. With two months of back wages burning holes in our pockets it wasn't hard to have a good time ashore. One afternoon I decided to split for Kyoto and, packing my knapsack, I made for the gangway. Jake, Joe, and Charlie were also going ashore. The old-timers looked at me with disapproval, asking "Are you going on the town looking like that?"

I had on my basic blue jeans/work shirt outfit and hadn't really given it much thought. Seamen, however, like to dress up when going ashore. They carefully unfold their special outfits and slap on their cologne (and not Old Spice, either—Jimmy said all anybody gives him at Christmas is Old Spice gift sets!). It was a way of distinguishing themselves, I guess, but they all had the worst taste in clothing. Billy especially—when he got ready to go ashore, he inevitably wore the tackiest polyesters known to man.

Charlie, on the other hand, was like me in that he didn't care what he wore. He started laughing at the old-timers and told them to go fly a kite.

After another tedious forty-minute launch trip the four of us walked into town together. Sakai was a very quiet little town, and we were probably some of the only Westerners who had visited there in years. The townsfolk treated us with something bordering on suspicion, serving us with a surprised and uneasy look in their eyes. In the center of town was the bank where we went to change our money. For some reason it took Jake and Joe an extra long time to get it done, so we told them we'd meet them in the bar across the street.

As soon as we were outside, Charlie asked me what I was up to. When I told him I was on my way to Kyoto, he asked if he could come along. We decided not to wait around for Joe and Jake—they were going to slow us down, and we were on the move.

The train ride was more like a subway ride from Coney Island to Co-op City. There were only occasional hints of something other than the urban sprawl. The cityscape changed, though—the imposing concrete megabuildings of Osaka gave way to smaller, less impersonal structures. Then there were the pagodas. Then the massive temples. We were in the heart of the former capital of one of the great aristocracies of all time.

We walked out into the street and took a look around at the swirl of traffic and tourists. Even in their own country, Japanese tourists march in large, controlled groups and wear cameras. And this was the tourist mecca of the whole Honshu Island. They visited in droves.

We decided to check out the big temple opposite the station. It was actually a complex of temples sealed off from the din of the modern world by a ten-foot earthen rampart that had no visible gaps in it allowing for comings or goings. This mystery could not go unsolved, so we searched for an opening. Sure enough, there was a private driveway, and we were in.

All we could hear inside were the sounds of the local birds and the distant hum of a hundred monks chanting. We had stumbled into the private sector and had the run of three great temples and their gardens. The broad wooden boardwalks creaked with each step—"the nightingale's song." It was intentional. If anyone ever tried to sneak up on the shogun, he'd be betrayed by his own treacherous footfalls.

The main buildings and court were open to the public. The Temple Prime was on that day filled with priests undergoing some sort of obscure Shinto religious ritual. Charlie and I took off our shoes and sat down before the meditating monks. The sound of their chanting was as smooth as the beatings of bees' wings. It drifted over the crowd and lulled us into a blissful calm.

But Charlie wasn't ready to spend the afternoon in a trance and got up. He wondered, "Where are the whores, anyway?"

We hit the street again and wandered the town.

There wasn't much to do at that point; we had reached something of an impasse. Charlie wanted action and I wanted temples. But I went along with him—why not?

Down the streets we roamed, always on the lookout for a geisha house or a promising bar. At one street corner we ran into a Dutch hippie and rapped with him for a while. Charlie scared him off, though, by asking about whorehouses. I guess they hadn't put that in *Let's Go: Japan.*

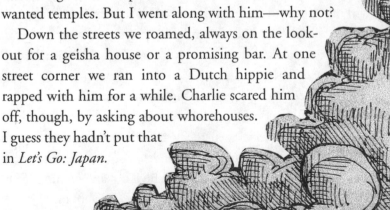

There was one building that advertised beautiful women on the outside, and Charlie dragged me in. The ultramodern and ultrachic décor should have tipped us off right away that we were on the wrong track. The elevator doors opened on the top floor and we found our bedraggled, sweaty selves staring at two high-priced, high-fashion models attending a very elegant dinner. We didn't bother with the other floors.

Night was falling and Charlie was disappointed by the lack of action. Even so, we were having a good time and decided to hit the road again. Suddenly we found ourselves in the red light district.

Charlie was psyched. This was the place—this was going to be it. But it never happened. The hawkers in front of every club either ignored us or said we weren't invited. Something was definitely not quite right, and it was us. They didn't want us hanging around, two uncouth Americans, strangers in the town, eager for their women.

We wandered the district for an hour or so before finally giving up. Charlie was angry and disgusted. So we decided: When in doubt, go to the closest beer vending machine (right next to the contraceptive dispenser and the Vend-O-Toy) and down a few beers.

As the night wore on, and as we grew less coherent, the better time we had. We took in the silent backstreets of the city, where front doors were never locked and every family garden looked like a work of art. We gazed up at the Toji Castle, dangling our feet over the moat and teasing the two-foot carp. And eventually we were reduced to hysterics, rolling on the sidewalk with tears pouring down our cheeks as the uncomfortable passersby gave us wide berth.

The night was spent in an empty house that was under construction. Charlie had obviously been out on the street before with no place to live, for he spotted the house at once and slipped in with a master's grace. It wasn't a long sleep, though. Charlie wanted to get out of there before the workers arrived. (It seems late-sleeping bums often get beaten to a pulp.)

Charlie split town that morning, wanting to get back to make some overtime. I stayed on and wandered up the mountain that overlooked the town. There I discovered several forgotten graveyards, and several more temples. The thick green underbrush that swept over them blended into the morning mist. There was a tranquility there that was lost even in the main temple down below, a simplicity and a quietude.

The TV had become the center of attraction on the *Rose City*. This was partly because we were sick of our movies, and partly because it was so weird. Each morning the day began with Tokyo TV's version of the *Today* show. In the lower right-hand corner a digital readout of the time let commuters know just exactly where they stood in the shape of the day's coming events.

In the afternoon it was all monster movies and serials. One prizewinner involved a record monster that threw 45s with deadly accuracy; others, various gymnasts in outlandish costumes.

One afternoon there was a samurai movie on. We were sitting around, watching it sleepily, when Bud came in and frowned.

"Where's the fucking monster?"

As if on cue, a huge fire-breathing reptile emerged from the lake and chased off the panicking samurai.

Perhaps the oddest shows on the tube were the baseball games. Every night there were at least two or three on. We did not find this altogether surprising, until the watchman told us that half the games we'd been watching were high school games. That seemed a bit much—broadcasting Yokohama High's big mid-season showdown with Osaka Academy. But the Japanese loved it, and, like everything else, they took it deadly seriously. At the end of a big doubleheader between two high schools, the losing team ran out onto the field and started filling little yellow sacks with dirt. We asked the watchman what was going on.

"Loser take dirt back to his home field and empty it out there so he won't forget he lose," he explained.

Throughout the year, TV stations signed off with the standard barrage of sappy music and soft-lensed shots of cherry blossoms. Sometimes. But this year was the thirty-fifth anniversary of Hiroshima, and there was a national observance. Each night on the tube photos of the atomic destruction were broadcast for five minutes at a time. That explained why they were so cold in Kyoto. It was August 7.

A new watchman was sent on board by the company, less slick than the first fellow, and not so well versed in English. I struck up a conversation with him and we ended up getting along famously. In a whisper he said he'd rig up the ship's telephone so that I could call the States for free, but I'd have to keep it under my hat—no one else was to know. There was an uncanny intuitiveness in this man; he seemed to have picked up on the story and crew of the *Rose City* right away. The officers were cold, and the crew was insane. He pointed out various members and asked me about them, as if he already knew the answers. In our final chat he asked me my name. He seemed to think he'd met me somewhere before. Oddly enough, I knew what he meant: There was something there that transcended the company.

When I say it was our final chat I mean anything beyond a nod. He had been on the ship only two days before he was taken off in a hospital boat. What happened is still unclear, but the results were obvious.

Ned was drunker than usual one night when he decided to go ashore. He stood out by the gangway and shouted all the Japanese curses his half-deranged brain could dredge up. When the launch showed up he jumped down onto the gangway and bitched at the launch crew. They took one look at him and refused to let him aboard, remembering the incident two days earlier when Jimmy was so drunk he'd fallen off the gangway and nearly drowned (he was trying to hang on to the three gallons of bourbon he was bringing back).

This refusal outraged Ned, and sent him into a fury. He ran up to B deck, burst into the cabin where the watchman was sleeping, and beat the shit out of him. The poor man managed to break free and get out of range of Ned's fists, but not before he'd been seriously injured. Ned was dragged off to jail by the harbor patrol.

I saw the watchman as he was leaving the next day. His head was in a bandage, his arm in a cast. I nodded to him and he nodded back. But that was it. He left the ship in silence, his head bowed. It was as if he'd been disgraced, publicly humiliated. The crew of the *Rose City* felt generally ashamed.

Although we had been in the harbor for a week and a half there was still no sign of fresh stores coming aboard. The food situation had become critical, and we were down to the last loaf of bread. Worse yet, our mail hadn't been delivered. This perpetuated great anger with the company. Not only was the crew on edge because they hadn't heard from home, but the lack of stores and mail made us think the company might be in financial trouble. That would mean they were probably going to pull what was known in the business as a Houdini act— declare bankruptcy and bail out of all outstanding debts and obligations. That would mean we'd get paid only for the work week—all our overtime would be lost.

But stores did show up, and we spent the better part of a day loading up. It was like something out of a Jerry Lewis or early Jack Lemmon movie. The crew members were all in good spirits, and the work moved in a parade of bad jokes and slapstick. The most enjoyable part of the whole day was bringing on the beer. The officers were resupplying the ship store with well over two hundred cases, and the crew readily formed a chain to relay the precious cargo up to the C deck lockers.

For now, however, the real thing was in the bars ashore. After we'd loaded up, I went over to Sakai with the cadet. He was off to see Kyoto, having heard of the adventures Charlie and I had. Pete had also gone, but by way of a hotel tour, a great opportunity to see the temples of medieval Japan through the tinted windows of an air-conditioned bus. I was beginning to realize that Pete was in fact an honest-to-god preppy.

The cadet and I soon found a bar and sat down to drink a few before we went our separate ways. I'd gotten high with him a few days earlier, along with Charlie and the third engineer. That was kind of nice, breaking the law with an officer, but the Third was a young fellow, and it wasn't particularly out of character.

The cadet was flying home soon in an effort to get back to the Academy in time for the fall semester. This trip was already taking longer than expected. We sat there, drinking in the calm Sakai afternoon, and reflected on the ship and what had gone down. It was the first open discussion I'd had with anybody, and it was a good release for the emotions. He surprised me; he was in fact a good-natured Wilmington boy who just happened to have nothing to do when he graduated from high school, so he'd signed up for the Merchants. I'd thought he seemed out of place; more than once I'd seen him gazing romantically off at the sunset, or watching a rainbow out at sea.

He also surprised me by talking about Billy. We'd all been shaken by what we'd seen the other night, but the cadet more so than the others. He was convinced Billy was a hopeless case. He also mentioned that Billy now thought I was all right. I'd learned to do my job, and I knew how to drink, so Billy was impressed. That was the best news I'd had in months.

We split up and I hopped a train for Nara, home of the Todai-ji, the great bronze Buddha, and center of the old religious oligarchy that predated Kyoto's preeminence. On the train I made conversation with a friendly Japanese businessman next to me. It was a good time. He spoke excellent English and was full of anecdotes about Osaka and Nara.

When we reached Nara, where the gentleman lived, he insisted that I accompany him to a Catholic mission a few blocks from the station. Not really sure of what to do, I followed. The mission was typically hideous 1950s modern and surrounded by a few miserable attempts at a Western garden. In the courtyard the man told me to wait and disappeared inside. I watched his progress through the plate-glass windows that covered the whole side of the building. He ran hurriedly up the stairs and into a music-filled room, where I could make out a number of people talking loudly. The man bent over to someone—they were all seated on the floor and out of sight—and then ran back downstairs. He put his shoes back on and joined me in the courtyard, saying the priest would be down to see me in a moment.

We waited about five minutes. The gentleman was getting nervous and was afraid I was getting offended at being kept waiting. Then a heavyset man wrapped in a white kimono appeared. To my surprise it was a peach-faced old Scot with a shock of white hair and a great accent who took my hand and shook it heartily. What was going on was that the Japanese gentleman had asked if I could stay the night there, since I'd mentioned that I'd nowhere to stay. The priest smiled benignly, but I could see that his lips were drawn back with uncomfortable tightness. I told him I was in the Merchant Marine.

"The Merchant Marine, eh? Well, then, you shouldn't have any trouble finding some lodgings! Well, good luck, lad, and enjoy your stay in Nara."

That was that, and the gentleman and I returned to the street. Before we said good-bye my friend handed me a pack of cigarettes and wished me well. We walked back to the center of town again and waved "so long." He disappeared into the throng of late-night commuters.

So, there I was, alone at night in Nara. I strolled into the Great Park and wandered along the pebbled paths and squatted down by the five-storied pagoda Horyu-ji. Crickets and strange Asian birds echoed all around the sleepy park. Occasional clusters of Japanese families and couples were the only interruptions to the stillness of the scene.

Eventually I ventured into the heart of the park. For some reason I was very nervous. It was exceedingly dark, and the forest grew thicker and more disturbing. I'd lost the sense of spiritual quest. This was a very different journey than those I'd taken in India. I wanted to find Zen bliss, but my mind was elsewhere, on the mundane, on the worldly, on the life of a merchantman.

Cringing at the strange calls of the night insects, I kept to the main path. Then I looked to my right and saw in the soft vaporous light a panorama of two hundred deer lying by a gurgling stream. I slipped around them as quietly as possible. As I moved, the primordial landscape unfolded like an ancient scroll. They were scattered among trees and rolling hillocks.

I stepped off the path and sat down against a tree. The deer were at first startled by my intrusion, but settled back down before long. I watched them for God knows how long, the fragile serenity of the scene hanging tenuously in the air. Then, to my amazement, a noisy family walked straight up to them without the least hesitation. A few of the deer stood up, but most of them simply watched. The yelling children handed out Deer Snax and laughed with glee. My Zen ink painting was suddenly a Kodak postcard, and I split.

I wandered the park some more, following the family's example and walking through the heart of the herd. The night continued to be foreboding and I decided to sleep in town. I thought the best way to approach the lack of shelter was to get as drunk as possible and find another vacant building to pass out in. I walked into a bar and got a beer.

Japanese bars are not like those found in the West. First of all, they don't serve drinks; they serve bottles. If you want whiskey you buy a bottle, which they tag for you and keep on the shelf. From then on you can go into the bar at any time and drink from your personal bottle. The other notable difference is that when you sit at the bar the geisha girls wait on you personally. They wipe the bar under your drink every three minutes, and if you've drunk a third of your glass they'll take your bottle and fill it to the brim again. At first it's somewhat intimidating, but after a while it becomes fun. Besides, just seeing the petite Japanese women, let alone having them wait on you, was a thrill for us all.

That night I chanced upon a lively local spot where no tourists were to be seen. The locals thought me something of a curiosity. I was wearing a traditional Japanese shirt I'd bought and was a six-foot-two white boy alone in an uncosmopolitan part of town.

They crowded around me, and the geisha tried to ask me where I was from. I drew a picture of the ship, and they all exclaimed in understanding and surprise. At least I wasn't another tourist. They then started talking all around and about me in a different tone, occasionally glancing at me. Every now and then I made out a word I could understand. Words like *American* and *Hiroshima*. I sat back and drank my beer. Shrugging at them, I tried to convey the idea that I hadn't even been a twinkle in my daddy's eye then. They continued the debate.

I decided to split the scene. The geisha asked me where I was staying, and I replied nowhere. They looked at one another with concern. I shrugged again and said good-bye to the geisha, who watched me disappear into the night with a melancholy stare.

I had trouble finding a vacant house. When I did come across a construction site I broke in and tried to bed down on the floor. But within ten minutes I felt something crawling up my back. I freaked and, jumping up, reached down my shirt and grabbed some slimy insect/snail-like thing and dashed it to the ground, then ran like hell.

My next attempt was in the backyard of an apartment building, but the mosquitoes were horrendous. I finally crashed out on a park bench in the center of town.

After a couple of hours the sun rose, and I decided to go see the temples. The deer had roamed into town during the middle of the night and were standing in the streets with impunity. A strange place, this was.

Too burnt out and tired to really appreciate the sights, I went through the motions like an automaton. I felt like I was attending a lecture because it was required. The Japanese loved it, however, and were out in droves. All the same cheap junk that fills Ocean City was being gobbled up by Mr. and Mrs. Executive-san and their three lovely children. Disillusioned, I went back into town.

I'd forgotten that the Japanese drive on the left and, stepping boldly into the street, I heard a horn blaring behind me—I'd looked the wrong way. A motorcycle skidded to a halt, smashing into me. I didn't travel very far and only received a few minor abrasions on my arm. The motorcyclist picked up his beautiful new bike from the street. In avoiding killing me he'd twisted the bike to a sliding stop, and now it was scratched and dented. He looked at it and then at me.

"Forgotten." That was all he said. Then he got back on the bike and rode off.

Ned was released and fined 41,100 yen for beating up the watchman. He was fairly unrepentant, and Billy acted as though he had done us all a favor. The others, especially the old-timers, did not agree.

CHAPTER 13

Back on the ship, after Nara, I returned to the tedium of gangway watch. True, I could read out there, but after two weeks of doing absolutely nothing except sit on the same uncomfortable crate, it was too much. One afternoon the 4–8 was the only watch on ship. I was doing Joe's sanitary work while Jake and Billy took turns at the gangway. They were even more sick of it than I was. Usually no one had to go out until the launch was expected.

Sweeping the corridors of B deck, I decided to take a break and look in on Jake. He was getting crocked, as usual, and called me into his room. Since our arrival, Jake and I had taken to sitting down with a bottle of Myers's Rum and polishing it off, a shot at a time, in a single sitting. This day Jake had some whiskey, some vodka, and a cooler of beer. Not long after we started, there was a knock on the door. It was Billy; he was sick of sitting out there and wanted a drink. So we drank.

And we drank.

And when we were through with the whiskey and the vodka and the beer we opened the gin. Then we heard a fateful knock on the door. It was the Chief.

Jake and Billy decided to pretend that no one was home. Unfortunately, we'd been making lots of noise, and Jake was so drunk that he was talking to himself while he was trying to hide, pretending not to be in his cabin.

Soon enough we had to come out, and Jake and I opened the door and faced the Chief. He had brought the Second down with him as a witness. He'd also woken the sleeping Bosun, who, as the head of the deck gang, had to be there. The Chief was livid; we were drinking on watch and had neglected our post at the gangway. He asked me who else was in there and I mumbled something about Billy under my breath. Jake denied it altogether, but it was clear the man was hiding inside. The Bosun ordered us out on the deck.

Billy didn't come out for a quarter of an hour. When he did he was too drunk to put up any pretense of innocence and joined Jake and me on the deck. There the Bosun chewed us out. Poor Dave—he'd been getting trouble ever since his stance on the sea watches, and he was furious that the three of us had stupidly played right into the hands of the Man himself. The Chief had something on us now.

That night the 4–8 watch went ashore to celebrate. So what if we were bad boys? We didn't give a care. Jake broke into song on the launch ride and Billy handed some money to a little Japanese girl who reminded him of his own three-year-old daughter, far away.

We didn't go far that night—just to the closest bar. It was an empty little place, frequented only by the townsfolk. We ordered a round of drinks and toasted ourselves for our heinous crime. We had become "brothers in crime" and loved it.

Jake looked over at the tape deck at the end of the bar. The other notable feature of Japanese bars is that they don't have jukeboxes. What they have instead is a library of instrumental tapes and a songbook. Anyone who wants to can sing into the house microphone to the music and entertain the patrons.

Jake got a fiendish look in his eye and asked them to turn it on. A minute later the 101 Strings were playing the theme to *A Man and a Woman,* and Jake was crooning away. He was in his element, and between the three of us the rafters were shaking.

We shifted anchorage on the sixteenth. They had finally found room for our oil and we were to pull into the dock and unload some of the cargo. Not all of it; we had to make another stop in Yokohama after this to unload the rest of the shipment.

The shift didn't take long, but the tying-up at the dock was a drag. Jake and the Bosun worked the winch, and it was left to Billy and me to do all the heavy work. But we did it, and we did it fast.

Seeing as this was our last night in Sakai, I went ashore and hitched a ride to Osaka for one final look around. I was by now familiar with the city. The mazes of the amusement district were no longer a mystery, and I could navigate to the various points of interest with minimal difficulty.

This time around I took a good look at the Japanese. They moved with an urgency that contradicted their smiling faces. There was always something to be done, and if you didn't do it first and best somebody else would. The competition was intense.

Their favorite pastime was pachinko. Pachinko is a souped-up variation of the original upright pinball machine. A player would buy a box of tiny silver balls and pour them into a feeder at the bottom, then hit a lever so that a ball flew up the track and bounced off the thin metal pins until it was swallowed up by one of the drains. Nine out of ten times the ball fell right through to the bottom. Sometimes the player got lucky and it was caught in a bonus hole and he got extra balls. But that was it. Nothing more, just extra balls, and the Japanese loved it. On any given street you'd see at least four or five of these parlors, and in each parlor there were hundreds of these machines, and at each machine there was someone flicking away, ball after little silver ball, hoping that maybe the next one would get him ten more to flick away.

As if this wasn't enough, their other favorite game was a variation on the groundhog and his shadow. Picking up a large mallet, one tried to smash the groundhog on the head as it popped up out of one of the ten holes in the game board. It was the physical alternative to pachinko.

Japan appears to have a totally Western culture, and it gave me the creeps to see how fast and to what extent they had begun emulating America after the war. They still hated us, that much was obvious. An old man spat at me in the subway, and their television was obsessed with the war and radioactive monsters. But everything still has a peculiar, singularly Japanese twist to it, right down to the airbrushed *Playboy*s and the porno movies that were all filmed from the waist up.

I purchased a few things before heading back to the ship. I had better memories of this place from five years earlier.

Sakai was all lit up that night; it seems there was a festival on. I delayed returning to the ship for one more walk of the town. The children were all dressed in traditional kimonos.

They laughed and giggled, led around by the hands of their parents. In the central square there was a carnival set up for them. A little pool of goldfish attracted the most visitors, as you could scoop them up in a net and take them home. One child looked up at me and started to cry—I guess I looked like an angry Kabuki giant to him.

Nearer to the dock there was a more subdued ceremony going on. I chanced upon it because I smelled clouds of incense wafting out of a side street. I worked my way through a sudden crowd of people, all dressed in traditional costumes. This chaotic swirl of people, smells, and smoke dispelled my unease with modern Japan: It was distinctly Asian. I bought some of the incense from an old man who squatted in front of a coal fire. Moving on, I came to a cemetery. The families of the dead were cleaning the graves and throwing sparkling water and flower petals before them. In the sky the full moon drifted in and out of the wispy clouds, and I returned to the concrete-and-steel maze of refineries.

The steward and the Bosun both asked me every time I returned from shore if I'd gotten laid, and every time I hadn't they were disappointed but still had a mischievous glint in their eyes. The two of them were alike in many respects. They were both big men who'd sailed the seas for years and had great tales to tell. Now, however, the Bosun was hamstrung by his health, and the steward by his color. The Bosun was the only member of the crew other than Pete and me to refer to him as "black" instead of "nigger."

That I hadn't gotten laid was not held against me. No one

had, except Spider, and that was attributed to the fact that he was Asian. As Joe explained it, Japanese women don't like Americans because they think we tend to be too well endowed. The best part of his theory was that he believed it sincerely.

We let go for Yokohama the next morning, after the shift to the docks. Again Jake and the Bosun worked the winch, and again Billy and I broke our backs towing and hauling the lines. The trip to Yokohama was only a day, and everyone took a day off, still drowned in a sea of booze. At least the new stores meant better food. When we reached Yokohama the next day, Jake and the Bosun worked the winch while, once again, Billy and I broke our backs towing and hauling the lines.

The night in Yokohama was a classic. Miguel, Ned, Billy, and I got off duty at eight and grabbed the first taxi into town. This town was more like it—the military bases had warmed the place up, as it were, and hungry seamen could get whatever they desired just by asking.

Our destination was the Seafarers Club. Merchant Marines are something of an international brotherhood. In every major port there's bound to be a club; just show your papers at the desk and you're in. Yokohama had an especially large establishment. In fact, the volume of shipping was so great in and out of Tokyo Harbor that there was an SIU hall nearby.

We pulled up in front of a splendid Deco building (that seemed to be the required décor of the Merchants). On entering, we found ourselves in paradise: a diner, pool tables, an English bookstore, a post office with a bank of telephones that had direct lines to the States, and a bar that looked a mile long.

Not being ones to dillydally, we set down to the business of eating real food and drinking as much as possible. Joining us was the new QMED from the Yokohama hall who had signed on as a replacement for our departed friend. He was a nerdy-looking fellow with big, thick horn-rims and a timid manner. Charlie, who had to work with him, seemed to think he was all right, but the rest of the boys didn't take to his reserved manner.

Tonight was no exception. While we were laughing it up, he sat alone, writing postcards. He was more out of place in this business than I was.

Joe, Jimmy, and Jake showed up an hour later. Amid shouts, we collected at the bar, and all seven of us insisted on buying the first round. It was quite a problem; with all the money we had, no one would allow anyone else to pay for anything. Such stalemates, after many threats and much verbal fencing, usually resulted in everybody paying and leaving the extra as a tip.

The waiters and hostesses thought this was all very unusual but did not argue with the ten-dollar tips for four dollars' worth of drink.

Billy jumped up and waved his screwdriver around, shouting, "Check this lineup out!" He was in one of his great trickster moods.

Meanwhile, Jake was angry about union business. We had only just gotten our mail, and Jake was livid. Venting his frustrations, he drafted a letter to the company expressing his displeasure. He also made a carbon of it, which he had me post in the club bathroom as a warning to other seamen.

The others nodded and agreed when Jake read it out in his exasperated whine, but they didn't think much of it.

After the bar, it was time to hit the pool tables, and Ned hustled us all. I came the closest to beating him, and he showed me respect for that. Out of the blue he bought me a pack of cigarettes and a beer. He'd forgotten the old animosity. We'd all gutted it out together, and this was the time to celebrate. He was one to follow Billy's example, and now that we were partners in crime I was all right in his book.

It was not one of those evenings when tremendous events shake the structure of the daily narrative. There were no major confrontations or outlandish escapades, other than Billy's christening of the ship with his beer bottle. And that was just it. We were all out on the town and having a great time together. In his role as Mr. Roberts, Henry Fonda (it figures) hit the nail on the head. His ship hadn't had liberty for over a year, and when at last they got ashore and tore up the town, he turned to his friend the doctor and said, "For the first time I'm working with a crew."

The doctor turned to him in surprise. "What do you think you've been working with?"

"Sixty-two separate guys."

And that's what that magic night in Yokohama did for the *Rose City:* It made us a crew.

The next morning we were all eligible to be declared Federal Disaster Areas. Billy and I moaned and groaned together on the watch, and when the Chief wasn't looking we drank some beers. I repeated Billy's adage: "Nothing cures snakebite like a little bit of its own poison." He smiled and we toasted each other.

We let go from Yokohama that afternoon. Jake and the Bosun worked the winch, while Billy and I broke our backs towing and hauling the lines.

In the evening the boys gathered for a good round of beer drinking. While in Japan, Ned had bought thirty cases of Asahi, insurance against running out again. There was barely room to move in his room, as he had used them to build a throne for himself.

While in Japan I had bought a boom box from an oil official who had a black-market stereo business on the side. He'd come on the ship with catalogs of some of the latest electronic equipment and promised delivery that afternoon. I tentatively agreed to buy one, but when he returned he had a monster of a box, and I couldn't resist. Charlie got even more carried away and shelled out $1,100 for a complete system. I borrowed some tapes from Tony and took the box to Jimmy's room, where we were partying, and turned it on. It wasn't long before we were breaking into a cacophony in accompaniment to the music.

Billy was again in a good mood. We were on our way to Sumatra now, and it wouldn't be long before we were on our way back to the States. He grabbed me by the shoulder affectionately and got the attention of the others.

"You should've seen us on the bow. Four fucking shifts in four days! Jake wasn't doing anything. We was busting ass! We were a team up there, a fucking team!"

It was true: By the fourth day, Billy and I worked in such sync that the job could be done in fifteen minutes, where it usually took thirty. Over and done with, we moved at rapid-fire pace without a hitch. We were a team.

The trip to Sumatra was only a week long and in that short time we had to Butterworth all the tanks again. On Thursday the twenty-first, our second day out, we had just gotten started on the forward three. The Bosun sent me in to make coffee for the morning break at about nine thirty. I used this as an opportunity to rest my dogs in the lounge for a few before going back out on deck. The chief engineer spied me and sauntered in, saying, "Quite a bit of excitement out there, no?" I thought he meant the Butterworthing and shrugged.

He raised an eyebrow and then realized I didn't know what he was talking about. "No, I mean about the submarine. The Russian sub that's on fire."

I stared at him and then jumped up and moved to the window. On the horizon were the dark outlines of airplanes circling over the open ocean. I ran out to the bow.

At 9:19 the bridge had received an SOS from a Soviet sub that said it was on fire, but that no American ships were to come to her aid. This was sixty miles off Okinawa, and only half an hour from our present position, so we immediately changed course and headed for the disabled craft.

On the bow the sight was clearer. Four planes and a helicopter circled over a small, dark silhouette. A British LNG (liquid natural gas) tanker—the most specialized and dangerous of ships on the seas, the gas having to be kept in massive holding tanks at subzero temperature to keep it from exploding with the force of an atomic device—had arrived on the scene a few minutes before and had weighed anchor, in accordance with the law of the sea.

As we steamed closer, the sub came into view. It looked small in comparison to the two supertankers. On the deck were the shrouded bodies of nine crew members who had died in the incident. Men in radioactive protective gear were running around the deck, shooting flares at the planes overhead in an attempt to keep them from photographing the ship. In the water, frogmen hovered about its screw, tinkering with it and diving under the hull.

Tony, Billy, and I stood on the bow and witnessed the spectacle. Something was not quite right, and it was obviously no small fire that had called out the nuke patrol. On the radio Pete heard reports of a mutiny, but it looked like something in the reactor to us.

When we got within two hundred yards, I yelled out, "Do you want any blue jeans?" and that started us laughing and offering Marlboros and silk stockings. But Billy quieted us down. It was a grim sight, and not one to joke about.

The British captain radioed that if there were any contaminated men he didn't want them. The Russians remained deadly silent. Two days later a Russian tug arrived and towed the crippled ship back to an undisclosed port on the north coast. This created a diplomatic incident: The tug had entered Japanese waters on its way home and outraged the Japanese. It was a nuclear-powered vessel, and the nation was still observing a state of mourning for the victims of Hiroshima and Nagasaki.

Today we finished Butterworth and passed a picture-postcard view of Bataan. We sailed due west for Dumai (Sumatra). It's Ned's birthday.

A lone swallow flew by, making me sad to see it so stranded. Squalls pass us from underneath monolithic and gargantuan rain clouds and thunderheads. Saw a double rainbow. Today we passed a deserted boat off Vietnam.

—8/22/80

CHAPTER 14

Boat people were still pouring out of Indochina at this time. Some of the crew had been on ships that came across floundering old tubs loaded with refugees and had taken them on board. As a rule, refugees were malnourished, suffering from exposure, and disease ridden. I shivered at the thought that the lone boat I had seen was a ghost ship, the haunted remains of a desperate flight to freedom that had fallen prey to the Indonesian pirates who combed these waters. I mentioned this to the Old Man, who replied that he wasn't going to take "any fucking boat people" on his ship.

Saturday night was the date of one of the gala events in the voyage of the *Rose City.* We were still overflowing with booze, and as it was such a warm and beautiful night out we decided to have the party on the stern. Billy, Ned, and I, joined off and on by Jimmy and Charlie, brought some chairs, a cooler of beer, and my boom box out on the deck and rechristened the *Rose City* the *World's Largest Yacht.*

We sang and joked unabashedly. Ned, on his own, took care to wrap my box in towels so the salt air wouldn't get to it. They were like that—clean, quick, and efficient. "An SIU ship is a clean ship," I was often told when someone would inspect the disarray of my room.

Jimmy was a master at pacing the party. He first had us play a Jimmy Buffett tape as a warm-up. The Florida hipster was a lover of the sea and sang about drinking, whores, and being out on the ocean. In a word—perfect. Jim also had a tape of Irish drinking songs that he wouldn't break out until we were all properly inebriated.

Tony was always one to improvise a tune. He joined us briefly and broke into an encore of his favorite work song, a little ditty about the officers.

We took turns singing and making up our own appropriate lyrics. Tony was making a name for himself with the boys. He'd been out of it for the most part, a strange, silent giant, but lately he'd been joining us, and the boys took a liking to him. It was a sense of self-preservation that had kept him from hanging out earlier; he knew better than to shoot his wad too soon. Now, however, we were a crew, and in these last few weeks, when we'd be getting ashore, it was all right to let loose once in a while.

The night was warm and splendid. The sea rolled by in smooth swelling waves, the moon reflecting off it like silver. It was a benevolent sea, warm and relaxing. We leaned against the rail, our heads back into the wind, and drank in the pleasure of it all. We were almost home free.

At midnight we shifted into the lounge because Jimmy had first standby. I brought the trusty box along and Jim deemed it high time to put on the Irish songs. They were an instant hit.

I'm a rambler and a gambler,
I'm a long way from home,
And if you don't like me
Then leave me alone.

I'll eat when I'm hungry,
I'll drink when I'm dry,
And if the whiskey don't kill me
I'll drink till I die.

The other big favorite was "The Wild Rover."

In our drunken glee we started wrestling and dancing Irish jigs to the sounds of the music. 'Twas merry. I did notice, though, that when he sang the first song Billy unconsciously changed the last line to "I'll live till I die."

Reentering the Straits of Malacca, we made our way along the north coast of Sumatra, Indonesia, to the mouth of the river that snaked its way inland to the port of Dumai. Once we made the big turn, the clear, blue water of the ocean yielded to the sickly-brown silt of the freshwater way. On the shore the dense rain forest stretched

across the horizon like a thin vibrating wire. There was not a hill to be seen—just hot, vast jungle. On the banks of the muddy water we could occasionally glimpse settlements, crude grass-and-driftwood shanties that housed dozens.

We waited patiently as the ship lumbered slowly inland. For a river not much wider than half a mile it was astoundingly deep. We traveled up it for the better part of a day, not reaching Dumai until mid-afternoon.

It could hardly be called a town—a mud hole amid the steamy miles of swamp and jungle perhaps, but not a town. There were a few large holding tanks, a small refinery and pumping station, and the crumbling remains of an unfinished dock. Farther in there was supposed to be a town, but it didn't look likely. We'd have plenty of time to investigate, however; we were going to be there a week.

Indonesia meant only one thing to me: Djarums. I craved them, I needed them, I hadn't had one in months and I was going crazy. The oil execs pulled up alongside our anchorage (until there was room for us at the dock, we were to remain on the hook in the river) and boarded the ship. Yes, we were clear for customs, and yes, we could go ashore. I jumped at this and hitched a ride with a fellow within fifteen minutes of our getting there. Bud, who was on watch at the gangway, was impressed by my eagerness.

The fellow with whom I was riding was a bit of a slickie-boy. He dressed in the same postmod way as every Asian from Bangkok to Taiwan who thought himself Joe Western Cool (that is, a cross between James Bond and Al Capone gone a-go-go). He had the Brylcreem hair, the cool dark shades, and the hipster jacket with open shirt and fake patent-leather shoes. He said he'd be returning to the ship in an hour and that I could go back with him.

We got out of the launch and walked down the boardwalk, past the discarded oil drums and occasional lazy locals to the guardhouse at the main gate. The exec said something to the two dusty soldiers, and I was waved on. There were upward of sixty people there to greet me, all wanting nothing more in the world than to fulfill my every desire. At once I realized I was back in a familiar Asia.

I waved them out of my way, smiling and joking with these Friends of the American Seaman. Arbitrarily I decided upon a young long-haired fellow and his less bright-eyed friends. They showed me to their bicycle rickshaw and ushered me up and in. To my surprise, one of the fellows climbed in with me. They explained that one rests while the other drives, and vice versa. Being a good ordinary, I did not point out that the one driving was now forced to move twice as much weight.

And in the sleepy sunlight the village purred. Dirt streets with echoing abysses for potholes, scrawny dogs and cats with broken tails running around between the goats and pigs that roamed the streets, naked children waving for baksheesh. I asked my friends, whose names were Ali (the longhair) and Tom-John, where I could get cold beer and some Djarums. At this they raised their eyebrows and smiled in surprise. "You like *kreteks,* yes? We show you good place."

We traveled down three of the five main streets and came to a halt in front of a neo–Frank Lloyd Wright hotel of standard Asian dimensions and entered. I stopped for a moment and purchased three precious packs of clove cigarettes from an old man squatting before a tray of cigarettes. My friends no doubt thought me crazy: Why would I smoke these things when I could smoke American cigarettes?

In the rear of the hotel was a lovely beer garden, surrounded by white stucco walls and shaded from the sun by the broad, flat leaves of an Indonesian palm. We seated ourselves at a table near the fountain. A slender young Indonesian girl wearing a single batik *ahoti* swayed up to the table. I ordered three beers for me and my friends. She returned with the drinks. My friends eyed me. "You like Indonesian girl, no?" Yes, but this afternoon we were here to drink in the cool shade and smoke savory cloves. I raised my glass and they voiced the traditional toast: "*Maramino.*" To your health.

The area around the Straits and the South Asian coast is by far the most dangerous in the world. Hundreds of ships disappeared there every year, not because of the weather or coral reefs—but because of pirates.

While we were upriver, the Old Man had us stand not only gangway; he also insisted that a man be on the bow to stand pirate watch. This was an exercise in futility—if armed bandits ever climbed up the anchor chain we'd either be dead or running like hell. Probably both. We had no way of communicating with the bridge, as they wouldn't give us a radio, and we had no way of defending ourselves. The Captain had a revolver, but probably never even learned how to load the damn thing. Thus Billy and some of the others broke out axes and large wrenches for our protection. We had every intention of running, but if worse came to worst it was nice to have an equalizer.

That first night was interminably long. We were all desperate to go ashore. When at last Joe showed up to relieve me I raced down to the gangway and joined Ned, Charlie, and Billy. We had this night coming to us.

The launch was run by nine- and ten-year-olds. They had mischief in their eyes and deft fingers in our pockets. The leader, who was all of eleven (I guess the owner was letting the kids do all the work), wore a cowboy hat and loved to point his finger at me like a gun and say, "Mafia!" They got us to the dock in no time, and the four of us were off and running.

As had been the case earlier that afternoon, there were hundreds of hustlers waiting for us. Charlie couldn't handle it and started screaming and throwing punches in the air as a sign for them to back off. I tried to cool him down; we definitely did not want to end up in an Indonesian jail. Billy and Ned, while not liking the crowd, either, didn't really notice it. They were running around like a couple of chickens without their heads, so psyched were they to get into a regular seedy port.

One of the dockworkers who came on the ship and changed our money into Indonesian rupiahs told us the place to go was Happy Gardens. It was the best whorehouse around, clean, and only a ten-minute drive away. Keeping this in mind, we set about trying to find a taxi or its equivalent. We walked to the central crossroads, still followed by a crowd of screaming rickshawmen. Charlie was going crazy, trying to outrun them, but there were just too many. We had to get on the road fast.

I saw my friend Ali and was discussing riding out with him when Ned and Billy called me over. They had hired an English-model '62 Chevy for the ride out to Happy Gardens. I said good-bye to my local friends, and away we went.

In addition to the driver there were two "assistant" guides who climbed into the front seat with him. The car revved up and took off down the Dumai Highway. Surf music played over the beat-up old tape deck in the front seat. Outside, the flat expanse of impenetrable swamp and jungle flew by in an eerie blur of silvery blue. The moon hung low and heavy in the hot night.

And true to the man's word, the drive took only ten minutes. We pulled into a walled compound through a crumbling iron gate that read HEPPI GARDENS and parked. This was the place. My stomach churned with nervousness.

"A whore is a seaman's best friend." For those who spend life within the unyielding and regimented confines of a ship at sea, the crumbling iron gate that read HEPPI GARDENS spelled out an all-too-infrequent chance for release and escape. This was the place. With sixteen hours a day, seven days a week, and twenty years' sea time to go before an ineffective union gave you a pittance of a pension, this was definitely the place. And as the rusted wreck of a car jerked to a stop and the Americans piled out onto the dusty street, the managers, women, and families who lived in the fifty-three brothels that comprised Happy Gardens were each hoping theirs would be the place.

The three guides jumped into action. So far things were rolling right along. Of the dozens of desperate rickshawmen back at the dock, they had scored the Americans. The next step was to guide these rich sailors to one of their contact whorehouses. If they could manage that, they'd be set: The Americans would spend their money, and they'd receive a healthy commission. Then there was always the additional chance of persuading the sailors to give them "lunch money" and a tip.

The Americans swaggered down the center of the street and hooted lustily. From the small two-story concrete houses on either side, the madams and their girls called out. Each house was the same: In the front room there were a bar, some tables, and a dance floor illuminated by a bare red light in the center of the ceiling, plus a few Christmas lights that blinked over the bar; in the back the girls lived in twelve tiny rooms to which the customers were ushered through a veil of nylon and plastic beads.

The guides were hesitant to force the issue of which house to go to, and the Americans marched triumphantly on through the compound. One aggressive madam sent out three of her girls to coax the sailors into her house. The friendly embraces of the girls were heartily returned by the Americans, one of them grabbing a girl under each arm and throwing his head back in laughter. But the victory march was not slowed, and eventually the disappointed girls let go of the sailors' bodies and, standing silently in the street, watched them disappear into the night to spend their dollars elsewhere.

Before long the Americans had run out of street and found themselves at a tollgate that sectioned off the far corner of the compound. The guides were agitated by the Americans' desire to keep going. Breaking their polite and nervous silence, they tried to convince the sailors that number 11 was the best house in Dumai. But the Americans were not to be thwarted by a roadblock as trivial as this, and in one great sweep of their arms they tossed the gate aside and pushed on.

The buildings and arrangements were no different at this

end of town, but the people were. The angular, dark faces of the Indonesians gave way to the round, olive profiles of the Chinese. What Mexicans and Puerto Ricans were to America, the Chinese were to Southeast Asia. They had spread out from the mainland to every country and island, bringing their money, their businesses, and their influence with them. But most of all, they brought racial tension.

The guides shifted nervously in the shadows as the sailors chose a house at random and entered. The Indian proprietor jumped up at the sight of three Westerners eager to spend their wages in his establishment. Ushering them to a table, the Indian signaled to the girl behind the bar, and immediately the room was filled with deafening generic hipster music of the sort heard only on TV cop shows.

The sailors set about the business at hand. From behind the veil a number of girls swayed out and, on request, brought a beer to each of the Americans. It was an arbitrary process so far as the Americans were concerned. They were far too excited to look over the entire inventory and accepted the specific girls presented to them without question. The Indian retired behind the bar. So far, so good; his patrons seemed pleased. Pity there weren't more of them, but at least his top girls would take in some money tonight.

The Americans responded to the girls in different ways. One grabbed his right away and slipped out back. The second giggled and necked with his, forgetting his wife and child, so far away. The third toasted his friend and turned his attention to the girl sitting in his lap. Having absolutely nothing to say to her, he nodded his head toward the veil. Acknowledging his desires, she led him by the hand to her tiny closet room. Closing the door, she went over to the tape deck and put on *The Hits of 1974!!* Turning around, she smiled at her customer and initiated her seductress act: Each eyelid became a long, flowing curtain behind which her opal eyes burned with a practiced fire; her hips swayed gently, erotically to the beat; her lips became full and pursed. She slinked up to the sailor and methodically undressed him, meticulously folding each article of clothing as it was peeled off and carefully putting it away. The sailor, once fully unclothed, lay on the foam rubber and plywood that were her bed and watched her strip. When not enfolded in her cheap silk dress, her figure lost its appeal. She had a tired body. Extra flesh hung around her waist and buttocks. Her thighs were worn from wear. Her trained hands showed the signs of someone who has worked too hard for too much of her life.

When the Americans had finished with their girls, they bargained as to the price. They said four hundred rupiahs, and the girls said a thousand. Six hundred became the settlement, and a round of drinks was bought for the house. It was time to strike out again, and, leaving a tip, the Americans bade farewell to the girls and the Indian and rejoined the one waiting guide.

He was pleased to see his charges and pressed the point that number 11 was the happening spot. The sailors were amenable to this, and so the four of them recrossed the frontier and marched through the Indonesian sector once again. The other two guides were leaning against the car and leaped at the sight of the Americans. They laughed and joked, getting a vicarious kick out of watching these sailors go to town, and keeping track of their locations, as the sailors tended to splinter off separately for horseplay during the walk up the street.

The mama-san of number 11 was Susie, a sensuous, lithe, dark-haired woman in her early thirties who carried herself with a Parisian sophistication. She welcomed the Americans and had one of her girls bring a round of Anchor beer. Seeing that they had successfully landed the Americans at their contact's house, the guides asked for some lunch money and left the sailors in Susie's knowledgeable hands.

The young ladies of number 11 were especially friendly that evening. It was clear that the sailors were here for the rest of the night, and the tension of the hunt was relieved. All collected at the table joked and sang, none of the run-down "business is business" attitude of the Chinese house tempering the fun. The sullen moroseness the sailors carried around on the ship was likewise dispensed with. Even the grimmest of the group behaved with good-natured abandon. He grabbed the girls and fondled them merrily. He laughed. He drank. In a slow, systematic stupor he became the king, and number 11 was his castle. Susie sat by his side, responding avidly to his attentions and setting an example the other girls could only hope to emulate.

Then one of the guides burst triumphantly in and stood to one side of the door. Gaining the company's rapt attention, he gestured flamboyantly and heralded in three newly arrived fellow crewmen. It became a house party. The stereo speakers blasted the new Japanese disco hit "Samurai," the liquor flowed in waves, and number 11 went wild.

One of the newcomers jumped up on the table and, ripping his shirt open, announced that he was awesomely well-endowed and that he was going to get it on continuously for the next six hours. Throwing his money away in a drunken euphoria, he found a girl to his liking and skipped off into the back. The others roared with laughter and applauded his conquistadorial spirit.

Before long most of the sailors had gone to the back. In the once animated barroom, two of the Americans and a few of the girls sat quietly, too woozy to go through the motions of festival. The music continued to blare just loud enough to kill any conversation between the sailors, and the English of the girls was just bad enough to kill any conversation with the two of them. They sat sipping beer, the dark red of the bar light pierced only by the steady, regular glow of Djarums and Marlboros being sucked on.

Susie noticed the dangerous lag in the volume of partying and from out back brought in some new girls to brighten up the situation. One was a small, petite beauty in her late teens. The other was a smiling half-Indian with a flipped Angie Dickinson hairdo and a sleeveless paisley dress. Apparently one of Susie's trademarks was her uncanny ability to choose the right girl for a customer, for moments later the two sailors and the girls were off to the back rooms.

Meanwhile, the other sailors were finishing up with their girls. One of them stumbled down the hall to the bathroom. The Bosun, who had never caught a dose in forty years of whoring, had advised all those going ashore to wash down afterward with alcohol and urine. Not wishing to pick up some strange tropical venereal disease, the sailor entered the five-foot-square bathroom and sanitized himself as instructed. In doing so he got a chance to look around. He was in what was basically a concrete box. In the far corner there was a small hole for a toilet. But the complete lack of plumbing meant the wet floor he was standing on barefoot was . . .

In another room, one of the sailors and his girl were disturbed by a loud banging on the door. It was "the king," demanding a cigarette. A minute later the American in the next room banged on the wall. The sailor tossed a pack of matches over the plasterboard partition that separated the two rooms. Then the king returned and kicked open the door. He wanted to know where the sixth member of the crew was. The sailor told him to piss off.

Before long there was more banging on the door. It was Susie, shouting and laughing hysterically. The king had carried her upstairs and gone wild with her. She screamed that he was a crazy man, before breaking into more laughter. The sailor sat on one end of the bed while his girl and Susie sat on the other, discussing the king's exploits. Then, from down the hall the king came running. He burst into the room and leaped on Susie. The mate in the next room, hearing all the racket, showed up in the doorway with his girl. They stared in silent awe before breaking into laughter themselves. They weren't sure what the hell was going on, but they did know there were four scantily clad people rolling around in the same bed in hysterics. This was number 11: Susie's place. Tomorrow it would be a vague hangover, and next week maybe a painful disease. Tonight it was heaven.

In the course of the evening's merriment the whores and I turned the boys on to Djarums. They liked them, and I was vindicated.

Charlie decided to stay on. He had found the woman of his dreams and was in no mood to go back to work. Our guides collected us at three and took us back to the launch in time to return for our morning watch. It was not easy staying awake on the bow after an all-night party. If any pirates were in the area we'd just as soon let them take the bloody ship; we wanted to go back to Susie's place.

Once watch was over, I crashed immediately. I woke up in the afternoon and joined the crew in the lounge. Pete had gone to a whorehouse in town and caught a dose. In his four-summer career as a seaman he'd never done it before, but now that he was going to graduate he was not going to need to work for the extra money and felt he'd better get it under his belt, to say he had done it. He should have listened to the locals: Houses in town are bad news.

After the evening watch, I went into town by myself. I wanted to look around and see the sights without worrying about whores and drinking. On the dock I ran into my local friends. Ali was ready to show me around, but I said I wanted to take it easy. He could dig it, and with his trusty sidekick Tom-John he led me down the gilded streets of Dumai.

All the shops were open, bright lights and tinny music vying for attention. This was a black-market town—anything I wanted could be found, or at least a reasonable facsimile. I wanted some tapes for my box, and Ali showed me to a tiny shop that specialized in bootleg Western music. I found, among other things, Creedence Clearwater Revival's greatest hits and bought a copy for myself and Tony.

We sauntered around some more, Ali trying to copy my every mood and attitude. We went into a bar and I bought some drinks. I gave them some Marlboros and they told me how they, like everyone else in this town, had come from the mountains to work for the oil companies. Some found work, most didn't.

Leaving the bar, we wandered some more. I was definitely into this, a nice quiet evening in a strange Asian port. Ali bargained for me at another tape store, and I bought some more beers. He turned to me and said, "We may get you Americans pretty bad, but you should see what we do to the Germans and Japanese."

I asked him about pot but he said it was no good—a seaman had been picked up by the cops a month ago, and there was a general crackdown. I left well enough alone.

Eventually I had had my fill and headed back to the dock. They followed and had me try some of the local food from a smoky stand on the street. Just as I was getting to the docks they said there was a great whorehouse I had to check out. I said I wasn't interested, but they insisted. All right, I agreed. I'll check it out, for the crew.

I was fairly buzzed, and they led me by the shoulder down a side street. It was empty, and at the end there was only total darkness. I didn't really think about what they were up to; I just decided that I was in no mood to go to a whorehouse and abruptly turned around and headed back to the main street. They stood there for a minute and did a double take, then hurried after me. Are you sure? It's a good place, lots of beautiful girls, yes.

No dice; I wanted to head home to the ship. They followed me to the dock. As I passed the squatters at the main gate, Ali asked for a thousand rupiah, for "lunch." Having just treated them to a night on the town, I was miffed. This begging business could go too far. I'd seen it in Delhi: Some unwitting American starts doling it out, and soon he's swamped. I refused.

Ali started to become more forceful in his demands. I continued to refuse. By now he was being followed by a dozen or so squatters and was picking up more as we walked. He asked me again in an angry tone. I pointed out that I had treated him and Tonto all night long. He didn't care, and his price went up.

I climbed down off the dock and into the launch, where two of the kids were sitting. It wasn't scheduled to leave for the ship for another hour, and I was going to have to wait. On the dock above, Ali and his friends, some twenty-five of them by now, collected. I still refused to give him money, and he shouted that I was an asshole.

I sat silently on the deck with the two kids. They were nervous. Suddenly a huge rock hit the deck and shattered in front of me, missing my head by inches. I looked up and saw Ali glaring down at me.

"You have friends? I have friends. You have knife? I have knife. C'mon, let's go, we fight."

I stared up at him. He had drawn a knife. His crowd gathered closer. Then a miracle happened, and the divine agents were Miguel and Joe. Just as the tension had reached the snapping point, the two of them showed up on the quay, grogged out of their minds and singing at the top of their voices. As

Ali and the gang turned their heads in unison to see what the racket was all about, I skirted along the underside of the dock, beneath my foes, and scrambled up on the quay to join my mates.

Ali and company were frozen with puzzlement. This was an unforeseen factor. Now I, too, had friends, and I was not trapped on the launch. It was deus ex machina at its finest.

In a minute I told them what was going on. Miguel was too drunk to hear, but Joe, through his bloody eyes, showed a limited comprehension. Meanwhile the kids had silently punted the launch over to where the three of us were standing and anxiously ushered us into its tiny cabin. The captain, my eleven-year-old friend, told me to stay inside unless I wanted "monkey business." I complied.

It was an odd stalemate. Ali and his friends collected at the dock nearest to us. The kids had moved the launch out of reach, but still wouldn't take us until the proper time. So we were trapped in the cabin, sweating it out.

Miguel promptly passed out in the bow. Joe and I sat up, watching as best we could the dark figures on the dock. Every now and then they'd throw a rock at us.

The cool blue-white glare of the streetlights reflected off the water and played on the roof of the cabin. Joe was reflective. I asked him why he'd never gotten married.

"Oh, hell, I was married once, but . . . it didn't work out."

We waited in the tense night. The kids were getting worried and decided they'd best get us out to the ship before trouble started. On the way out, I asked Joe if he'd ever smoked pot. He smiled and said, "Show me a sailor who says he hasn't smoked pot and I'll show you a fucking liar!"

On the dock Ali faded from view. I realized I couldn't go ashore again and expect to come back alive.

With my escapades in town I achieved a new standing with the crew. I was indoctrinated into the right sacred order of the DSL (Dumai Shit List) and became the subject of quite a bit of talk. The crew was outraged that the "motherfucking gook ragheads" would try a stunt like attacking one of the crew. They were also glad to see I had come out of it all right.

The morning watch after the incident was a long one. It didn't get light until seven or so, and I was still jumpy. Billy missed the first two hours, showing up in the launch at six, drunk and full of song. He was enjoying himself too much at Susie's to return on time.

In the afternoon I saw the kids again and asked them what was up. They said Ali was waiting for me. In short, they said that to go ashore was suicide. This was a town where you could get a man killed for ten dollars. Only two weeks before, a Korean sailor had been found drowned, presumably for his Seaman's Papers, which sell for as much as $1,000 on the black market. Seamen made good money, and these people were desperate.

Resigned to my river exile, I took watches for some of the others so they could go ashore. The bow at night was a quiet and foreboding spot. It was raining a lot now and I rigged a makeshift tent in the anchor block to keep us dry. With every bump and clang of the ship I jumped. I had visions of Ali climbing up the anchor chain with a knife firmly wedged in his teeth.

Conrad's *Heart of Darkness* kept me company. I read in the pale port light, trusty ax by my side. The wail of the mullahs echoed across the endless jungle that stretched out on either side of the river. Foot-long bats chased huge flying insects overhead. In the dark alleyways of the shimmering town across the water menacing figures preyed upon human quarry.

The next morning the crew was all charged up. Jimmy was so drunk on pirate watch that he had stumbled and fallen down by the hawse pipe. How it was that he didn't fall right through to the water and kill himself was a mystery. He was also so drunk that he stood the rest of his watch without realizing the damage he'd done to himself, for the next morning when he was sober he couldn't walk.

That wrote Jimmy out of the rest of the voyage. As soon as we got to Singapore to pick up bunkers (fuel for our engines), he was going to be flown home. That suited him just fine; he had a girlfriend he was dying to see.

True, Jimmy had been in the whorehouse, but seamen had ways of rationalizing that. As Jim himself said, "My tubes are getting rusty; gotta clean 'em out."

The other major event of the night was Miguel's brawl ashore. When I came off watch and went into the lounge, Miguel and Ned were the center of a controversy, and the Mexican was jumpy. I asked Miguel what the hell was going on.

"I don't know. I think I coulda kill somebody. Motherfucker starts trying to start a fight, so I hit him."

I sat Miguel down and asked him to tell the whole story. Miguel may have been one of the best-intentioned and kindest people I'd met, but he had a temper that would pop the pennies off a dead Irishman.

"I go with Ned to Happy Gardens last night, and that place we were before, when this cocksucker start banging on my door and asking for money for lunch. I'm from Mexico and so I say sure and give him some, but the motherfucker comes back five minutes later asking for more. I tell him to be quiet, the girl had a little baby in the corner of the room. He starts yelling at me, so I say sure, I give you money. I put on my pants like this and BOOM! I give him a left hook and BOOM! I hit him with my right. The motherfucker goes down like that. So I piss on his head." He started laughing at this point. "I run to Ned and say, 'Ned, Ned, I think I kill somebody.' And we get out of there. But then the cops come and stop us. They take a look at the motherfucker and say no problem, he is a troublemaker." Miguel was getting all worked up, reliving the experience. "Goddamn long-haired motherfucker."

Long-haired?

I asked Miguel to describe him.

"He was a tall guy, kinda like you. His name was Ali, or some bullshit like that."

I burst into laughter and, jumping up and down, told Miguel it was the same guy who'd tried to knife me the night before. Miguel looked at me with a huge grin on his face. This was even better—now he'd nailed two birds with one stone. The rest of the crew was equally pleased, and all that day there was a celebration.

But not for everybody. Billy was in an angry mood. He was

tired of the ship and was worked up about his wife and kid. He started drinking in the early afternoon. He was in the lounge when the Chief showed up. Billy had had enough. He started telling the Chief a thing or two in a loud and bitter voice. It wasn't long before he was shouting at the Chief. And the Chief loved it. He stared at Billy and egged him on, saying, "Yeah! Oh yeah?" He hated Billy and was baiting him. Jake jumped up and got between them. Billy was going wild and started jabbing the mate with his finger. Jake pushed the mate aside and forced Billy out the door, while the Chief stood there, waiting and baiting, sticking his pudgy Kentucky face out and sneering. Just as Jake slammed the door shut, Billy let go with a right hook that connected with the wired-glass window between him and the Chief. Jake led him, screaming, back to his cabin.

The Chief was very pleased with himself. He'd almost managed to get Billy to strike an officer (which would result in the confiscation of his papers by the Coast Guard), but threatening an officer was good enough. He turned to me and Jimmy and said, "You're witnesses."

We looked at him and shook our heads. "Didn't see a thing, Mate."

So Billy was in trouble. That afternoon I was called off standby and ordered to report to the gangway. The Chief said Billy had left his post. He was there, but he had fallen asleep behind the king post. The Second was brought out as a witness. The Chief wanted as much support as possible for the upcoming case against the troublemaker from Philadelphia.

We shifted from the river to the dock at nine that night. For some reason the Indonesian dockworkers were the most uncooperative people in the world. They absolutely refused to hear us or do anything they were supposed to. This made for strong feelings on both ends of the sea lines.

In order to get a line down to the tugs or the stevedores, a thin rope is attached to the eye of the line. At the end of the rope is a "monkey fist," "or monkey ball," a four-inch Gordian knot. Gathering up the thin rope in one hand, the seaman swings the monkey fist like a sling and casts it to the desired spot. The worker at the other end can then pull the rope and grab hold of the line.

Bud was especially good at this. When the Indonesian tugs were maneuvering us into the port and calling for the lines, Bud took careful aim. Just as we were closing in, he came running up to the bow. "Ha! I got a fucking gook right on the head." Everyone laughed heartily.

We worked until four in the morning, and then Billy, Jake, and I had to go on watch. The dockworkers were so frustrating that we were spitting and yelling obscenities at them as loud as possible. They returned the sentiments in kind. Finally, after twenty-eight hours of work (I'd been doing overtime), the cargo lines were hooked up to the manifold and we could catch some sleep.

We let go in the afternoon, but as it was getting dark we anchored in the river overnight; after we'd had it fixed in Japan, the radar had gone on the blink again. Even our captain wasn't ready to navigate the sandbars of inland Sumatran waterways at night.

On the bow, Jake and the Bosun worked the winch, while Billy and I broke our backs towing and hauling the lines.

Singapore. 1°17'N 103°51'E. Aptly deemed the "Crossroads of the World."

It took half a day to get there from Dumai. We anchored in Tanker Alley and waited for bunkers. The ship was only going to be there for eighteen hours.

We leaned on the rail and watched the sun reflecting the shimmer off the buildings in town, two miles distant. It seemed a shame to let it go to waste. We had buckets of money and we were sure that the friendly natives of the island would be happy to take it off our hands.

The Bosun said something about a supply launch coming up that evening. I turned to Tony, and he turned to Billy. Billy turned to Ned, and Ned turned to Miguel. Miguel turned to the steward, and the steward turned to Spider. Spider turned to Charlie, and Charlie turned to me. It was decided then: We were going to jump ship and go ashore, just to see the sights.

Loaded with money and beer, we piled into the launch as soon as it arrived and sped away from the ship. The night was just settling and the boat was fast. We were ready to go.

After a forty-minute ride we arrived at Singapore Station and jumped onto land. Taxis were awaiting us and, dividing our numbers, we secured two rides and told the drivers to take us to where the action was.

Now, *this* was a town. These people were fast paced, well oiled, and out for a good time. In the careening cars we taunted one another, each cab trying to overtake the other. Ned mooned our car out the window. One cheek read U.S. PRIME GRADE BEEF. The other read YOUR NAME. The reason for this was so that he could go up to chicks in bars and tell them, "I've got your name tattooed on my ass." And when they didn't believe him, he'd drop his pants and show them.

The taxis pulled up in front of a modern house somewhere in the suburbs of the city. It was, according to the drivers, the best place in town. No surprise—they were getting a commission, so as far as they were concerned no joint could beat it.

We went upstairs and were greeted by a friendly Indian gent with a waxed mustache and a flair for entertaining his customers. He sat us down on some couches and brought us beers.

We were waiting, not really knowing what was going on, when Papa-san returned. He stood to one side of the room and, with a sweep of his hand, ushered in a lineup of some twenty girls, all for the taking. We felt like Arab viziers at a slave market, sitting back on our cushions and sipping only the finest ambrosia.

Unfortunately, these girls looked like the cast from *Night of the Living Dead.*

Billy eyed Papa-san suspiciously. We had seen some Swedes in another room with good-looking girls. But, thinking quickly, he pointed to the best-looking of the bunch and called her over to his side. After a bit, the others chose partners. I just couldn't bring myself to do it; this was a bit much. Before long I was left alone in the room with the steward and his girl (a heavyset black woman slightly younger than he was), who were going to eat dinner. The stew was a romantic at heart.

Papa-san was flustered by my refusal to take any of the girls. He told me to hang on and disappeared. Moments later he returned with a beauty. She looked at me and rolled her eyes; I was way under her league—she was a high-class hooker. But Papa-san made the rules around here and made her get me a beer. She found this highly dubious. She returned with the beer and a scowl. I told Papa-san I wasn't interested. She made a nasty face at him, as if to say, "Why are you wasting my time? I told you so." He in turn frowned at me. Miguel had come on the scene and said the kid wants a nice girl. Papa-san split.

Miguel and I drank a beer together. He was concerned—didn't I want to get laid? I shrugged.

Tony returned, all smiles. He described his exploits and lit up his pipe. But the good time was not to last for long. The steward had left to get some food, but returned to say that Billy and Ned had gotten into a fight with Papa-san. It figured; they could start a fight in an empty room. Tony, Miguel, and I went downstairs and found the two of them waiting outside. Billy was incensed that the girls wanted to go drinking and dancing first, and Ned was infuriated that he couldn't make them perform certain sexual positions.

Not wanting to beat a dead horse, we jumped into a taxi, leaving Spider and the steward, and told our driver to take us to another place.

After a two-minute ride we stopped before a similar-looking building, only this one was more run-down. We went in and were ushered into a bare room with a single red overhead light and a few pieces of shabby furniture. We looked at one another dubiously.

The proprietor brought in three pathetic girls with faces like ten miles of bad road. There was no way. Ned started demanding other girls. The three ladies were ushered out, and a new one was brought in. Ned smiled and said he'd take her. They disappeared into a room across the hall. The four of us sat there, wondering what to do. We didn't want to wait around for Ned all night, but we couldn't spoil his fun.

Just then a nice young fellow came into the room. He was remarkably cheerful and seemed to live in the place. He asked us if we needed anything, to which Miguel replied he wanted some food. The fellow knew just the place, only a few blocks away. Within a minute we were off into the night.

The town was a strange mixture of Oriental and European, with broad, well-paved avenues lined with small huts and hawkers. The eatery where we ended up looked like a Parisian café—tiled, beautiful brass fixtures, and spotless—but was filled with families and old men hunched over squid tempura.

We sat down at a table and let our guide and Miguel do the

ordering. Frogs' legs, chicken breasts, spring mushrooms. We were living like kings. At one point in the meal we looked up to see the Indian from the first whorehouse stroll in with a stunning woman on each arm. He was as surprised to see us as we were to see him, and waved hello. We laughed—not even Billy could hold a grudge tonight.

It was two in the morning when we returned to the whorehouse to get Ned. I waited with Tony and Miguel outside while Billy dragged him out of bed. An odd little shrine stood by the front door. In front of a picture of the Buddha were an incense burner and a stack of paper money. They were printed with HELL BANK NOTES, CURRENCY FOR THE OTHER WORLD.

We gave our friend a tip. He was a little taken aback and didn't really want it; he was just being friendly. Saying good-bye, we grabbed another cab and went in search of a hotel. The Imperial had been recommended to Tony, and although I suggested Raffles, I consented.

We swaggered through the smoked-glass doors and entered the ultra-deluxe modern lobby. Tony and I took control of the room situation: "Yes, that's right, my good man, we'd like two of your finest rooms. Right, then. Have a good evening."

Sneaking Miguel, Ned, and Billy upstairs in the back elevator, we cruised the top floor and let ourselves into one of the rooms. Ned stood there openmouthed.

"I've never seen anything so beautiful. Look at this place! Can you believe it?"

I immediately went to the refrigerator and opened her up. My mates were speech-

less; there was a fully stocked bar, anything we could ever hope to drink.

We set to work. Billy and Ned were still amazed by the surroundings. The closest they had ever come to luxury before was the Olympia Movie Palace in North Philadelphia. They jumped on the beds and started hooting. Tony mixed the drinks.

The party continued for hours. I noticed that Miguel had disappeared and looked around for him. I found him curled up with a pillow in the closet. I asked him what in the world he was doing and he replied that he was tired but didn't want to spoil the party. Ned walked him over to the other room.

Miguel was going to get up in time to make it back for his watch, but the four of us had unanimously decided to blow it off. Let the Old Man take a piggyback ride on a buzz saw.

Tony was in fine form. Ned and Billy had never really seen him in action, except for the one time when we were doing the jigs in the lounge. Tonight he was completely out of control, sending Billy and Ned into tears of laughter. He pranced about the room and made the balcony his stage, shouting at the buildings across the way.

My steam finally ran out and I crawled into one of the beds. Billy shook me and asked me if I was okay.

"Are you all right, Monahan? How you doing? You goofy motherfucker!" He patted me on the shoulder as if to tuck me in.

The next morning we awoke in a predictable fog. Miguel was already gone, and Ned had called the steam company and found out that the *Rose City* was not leaving until after four. Hell, that gave us plenty of time—we could catch the 3:30 launch and make it back for the afternoon watch.

I made it clear that what we were to do today was to drink the original and quintessential Singapore Sling. This was agreed upon and we struck out. Our friend from the night before said the Jockey Pub was the home of the Sling. This sounded erroneous to me, but the others insisted. Again I wanted Raffles, but majority ruled.

After some negotiations we grabbed the fastest taxi and found ourselves in an exquisite Victorian pub. We settled ourselves down at the bar and ordered four Slings. The publican poured the rose-colored elixir into four tall glasses placed before us. It was magic.

Delighted at the success of our mission, we promptly ordered another round. I was leaning on the bar when I heard a grunt behind me. I turned around to see a bear of a man looking at me from a couple of seats down. I said howdy-do.

He was an American. Well over two hundred pounds, he sported a great bushy beard and smoked Lucky Strikes and drank Jack Daniel's. As we got to talking, I found out that he worked on the oil rigs all over these islands and lived in a bungalow just outside of town. He was an excellent character who lived the kind of carefree life we only dreamed about. He had all the advantages of the merchantman, without being out to sea for months at a time. He lived in a town populated by Australians, Indians, Chinese, Malaysians, Brits, and every other nationality on the seven seas. I asked him about Singapore Slings and he shook his head. We were in the wrong place; Raffles was the home of this peerless concoction. We rose to the occasion and bid the gentleman adieu. We had important business to attend to, and commanded the next taxi we saw to take us to Raffles Hotel, on the double.

We were greeted by a white colonial façade with lush tropical plants flourishing before the impressive colonnade. The smart Rajasthani doorman ushered us up the Persian carpet. Within the cool halls, the marble floor led past the Joseph Conrad Room and into the Long Bar. The potted palms swayed to the motion of the fans gently swirling overhead. A turbaned waiter carried in his white-gloved hand a silver tray of crystal cocktail glasses, each filled to the lip with a rich blend of Beefeater gin, Triple Sec, Bénédictine, orange-lime-pineapple juice, and Angostura bitters.

We leaned back in the wicker lounge chairs and ordered more rounds.

The ride back to the launch is not very clear in my memory. Of the four of us, Tony was the only one lucid enough to coordinate our getting back to the ship on time.

We spotted the launch in the crowded marina by the company flag she flew. The men on board said she wouldn't be leaving for another hour, so off we went to a seafood restaurant right on the water. There was an oversized fish tank next to our table that served as a foil to our pranks.

Once we were on the launch, the two employees sat us down in the back and took her out to sea. Ned passed out in the cabin while the rest of us lolled our heads to the rhythm of the waves.

From my seat I spied the flag waving from the mast over the pilothouse. There it was, the company insignia. It was too good an opportunity to pass up. While Tony and Billy acted as lookouts from their seats, I crept up on the roof and unhitched the flag from right over the pilots. The mission was a success.

Billy decided that was a good idea, and responded by throwing the life preservers overboard. The pilots saw him, however, and turned around to pick them up.

When we reached the *Rose City,* the Bosun was at the gangway, waiting for us. It was just four o'clock, and though we'd missed the morning's watch we were back in time to let go the ship. But there was a slight complication: The ship had been scheduled to leave at four. We had been sadly misinformed.

I turned to immediately upon boarding and went with Dave to the bow to hoist anchor. Billy and the others retired to the house. This was yet another mark against us. The old-timers were especially annoyed at Billy and Ned for being the worst performers on the ship. And the old-timers didn't take to the idea that I was one of Billy's running mates now. They thought he was a bad influence on me.

We hoisted anchor and let go for Borneo. Two and a half weeks and we'd be back in the States.

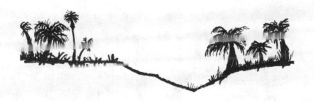

CHAPTER 15

THE TWO HOURS we delayed the ship cost the company
$2,000. Billy was too drunk to go on watch and asked
Tony to stand in for him but the Chief had seen him from the
bridge and knocked him off before he had a chance to report
the substitution. Another strike against Billy Mahoney.

The next morning the Chief filed a report against Ned and
Billy in the official ship's log. It was now in the hands of the
Coast Guard inspectors, who'd be reading the log upon arrival. Tony and I, because we had missed only one watch and
were first-time offenders, each received a letter of warning. The
Chief said it was little more than a formality. In truth, it was a
political move on his part, as Tony and I were the only people
left doing overtime, and the ship still looked like an ad for
Rustoleum. He wanted to get as much work out of us as he
could before the Coast Guard inspection.

We got to Brunei, a small British protectorate on the north
coast of Borneo Island, on Friday. The story was that the last
monarch of the kingdom was lying on his deathbed when he
decided to name an English friend of his as heir to the throne.
Although it hasn't any cricket lawns of the quality of the other

colonial possessions in the area, it had held out against the saints and despots of the postwar era.

There was no legal reason we couldn't go ashore, as was the case in Angola, but the company "was unable to contract a shuttle service to the shore." This time we were a good three miles offshore and didn't even bother trying.

Only two people came on board the ship. One was a dark executive type and the other a vaguely Chinese worker who helped with raising the submarine lines and attaching them to the manifold. It was probably just as well we didn't go ashore; some of the crew, including Sam, the new QMED, had once, and from the sound of it Dumai was by comparison a holiday.

There were also the spiders. Huge three-to-four-inch hairy spiders. Gathering in groups of fifty or more, they spun communal webs as long as 150 feet, and 75 feet deep, in order to catch and eat large birds and animals.

It was a sweltering, humid day, and the sun beat down on us with a vengeance. Normally we'd only have to work at hooking everything up for a couple of hours, but the winch broke. This created major logistical problems, like how in hell we were going to haul the cargo lines up on deck. The engineers were called out but hadn't a clue as to how to fix the bloody thing. In the end the only alternative was to cross-rig the stern winch, running the cable 200 feet down the deck and splicing it with the broken machine.

It was heavy sledding, and we worked for seventeen hours in the heat without a single break. The dusty strip of green that was the shore looked inhospitable anyway.

I was leaning against the rail when the Old

Man ambled up to me. He rolled his unlit cigar in his mouth
and stared out at the steamy harbor.

"See that water out there?"

I nodded. It was a sickly green hue and filled with mold like
seaweed and algae.

"If the sharks don't get you the sea snakes will." He had a
wonderfully bleak way of putting it. He chewed on his cigar
some more before ambling away again. The blistering sun ob
scured him from view.

We got off work at nine p.m. and crashed. Tomorrow we'd
be moving on. Homeward bound.

The next day was almost as long. The winch was still broken
and it took hours to disconnect the cargo lines.

Normal procedure for the unhooking of the cargo lines in-
volves a "pelican hook." This is a device that allows the seaman
in charge of the operation to swing the line via the boom out
over the water and snap it free. It is safe and effective, in addition to being standard equipment.

Needless to say, the SS *Rose City* did not have one. To make
up for this, we were using a rope lasso to unhitch the lines. Billy
and I were in charge of guiding the boom out over the railing
and freeing the line. While I reached out and steadied her, Billy
worked the lasso. Then a swell rocked the boat.

The rope snapped and the cargo line crashed into the sea.
Before he could move out of the way Billy was struck full in the
face by the half-ton block as it ricocheted back over the deck.
He fell down screaming and went into convulsions, clutching
his face in agony. I jumped to his side and put a rag under his
head as a pillow. Then came the hard part. I gently grabbed
hold of his hands and peeled them back from his face, not

knowing if there was going to be anything left but a bloody pulp. It was incredible—the man must have been made of tempered Hyrcanian steel; the only visible marks were a large swelling welt on his right cheekbone and blood in his nose.

But I saw the block hit him, heard a sickening crack when it struck, and knew Billy was in a bad way. He was continuing to have mild seizures. I screamed to the second mate to tell me what the proper procedure was for shock, but our erstwhile medical officer stood there dumbly with his mouth hanging open. Dave knelt down on the other side of Billy, but the others, including the Chief, nervously sidestepped the issue. I screamed at the Second again—this man could be dying—but there was no response.

As if he had heard all this, Billy suddenly broke free of my hold and jumped to his feet. The crew stared at him in stony silence, as if Lazarus had risen. A couple of us tried to help support him but he tore away from our attempts. He had literally shaken off the blow.

The Bosun had somebody walk him back to his cabin. He was still in great pain and had trouble walking on his own. And before he'd even reached the house, the Captain gave the orders to move out. The Old Man knew what had happened, but he was damned if he was going to delay sailing so a helicopter could fly out and take Billy to a hospital. He was a company man, and there was a schedule to keep.

None of us could believe this latest show of indifference. A man might well be dead in a few hours and the Captain was thinking in terms of percentages and assets. As we were casting off, we heard the Old Man yell over the Chief's radio that we were a bunch of pansies for jumping out of the way when the sea lines tightened. So what if they could snap and cut you in half; this was a ship, and ships had to move out fast and efficiently. He had already lost one man when Jimmy was flown home in Singapore.

We made the big turn today, out of the Philippines and into the Pacific. Straight across.

—9/7/80

As humorous and celebratory as Jimmy's injury was, Billy's was grim. For two days there was quiet on B deck while Billy lay in his darkened room with Jake and the Second watching over him. Jimmy had been bruised in a drunken fall and used the excuse to threaten to sue the company and be flown home to his girlfriend. Billy was struck by what should have been a fatal blow and by a quirk of fate survived. We had no way of knowing if he had a concussion or other complications. Head injuries are the worst kind.

Meanwhile, the deck department was now reduced to seven men. Joe and I were upgraded to acting ABs, and our respective watches split the disabled men's hours and pay. Injury was a way of life on the sea. After Billy's accident, Tony confided that the year before he had taken a dive from the Bosun's chair (a makeshift scaffolding used on the king posts and other out-of-reach spots). He was on his back for six months.

The Old Man was adamant in his decision. He'd show up on the bridge with his cigar, sunglasses, and potbelly hanging out of his open shirt. I kept to myself on the bridge, not carrying on the usual conversation with the mate on duty and speaking only when spoken to. There was a lot of tension building up.

My first day as acting AB, the Chief had me steer the ship through the Gulf of Leyte. There were only a few course changes, but we were on manual the whole time. I got my first taste of worming a supertanker through narrow sea lanes. The Chief said I did all right.

After a few days, Billy appeared to be recovered. He had an ostrich egg of a lump but was otherwise all right so far as we could tell. Jake was coaching him on how to get a good case against the company and had him feign complete illness for another day or so. It was a pleasure for them to have me go wake the Second whenever he was asleep and make him come down to check on some "new" ailment. If they were going to harass us, we were going to play the same game.

Ned, Billy, and I, as soon as Billy was well enough, made a practice of sitting in his room and drinking long into the night. After our adventures in Dumai, and especially Singapore, we were solid. Ned revealed his other tattoo to me: a multicolored

face of a monster that went from the base of his spine up his back to his neck, so that the horns curled over his shoulder and onto his chest. He said the pain of the needle was unbearable. I decided I was going to forgo the gold earring and get a tattoo of the rising sun on my right arm. It might not have been as classic as the Bosun's Popeye tattoo, but it was better than the fellow he told me about from another ship who had his fingernails pulled and LOVE and HATE tattooed on the soft skin underneath.

> *I didn't turn to this afternoon. I think the Bos was a little disappointed. Tony and I are the only ones left doing OT. Sugie-Sugie-Sugie. We're catching the tail end of a typhoon. God, sometimes the wait is suffocating.*
>
> —9/9/80

These last two weeks were nerve-racking and relaxing at the same time. Two weeks and we'd be in Seattle. That was all right, but even though we had come through it, we couldn't take it much longer. The old-timers took to reflecting with me on the old days. These new container ships, flag-of-convenience vessels, and the proliferation of licensed seamen in a dwindling job market had ruined it all for them. The good old days of the '50s were sadly lost forever, and they were just waiting to cash it in.

Above all, it was a lonely life. They kept telling me over and over to go back to school. "Get out of this racket. There's no future here. This is no way for a man to live." I had never seen people so depressed with the life they led.

Now was the time when they started thinking about seeing their wives and girlfriends again. Billy was desperate. His wife hung out with young, single secretaries when he was away, and he pictured her going off with them to some disco and meeting an available stud.

Bud had had a girl for two weeks when he got the job. He was mad about her, but the chances were she wouldn't be at the dock waiting to greet him with loving arms. Or anywhere else, for that matter.

The others, the old-timers, knew what to expect. The ones who were married would return home for a couple of months and then ship out again. The wife would deposit the allotment check and take care of the kids and the house while the husband was away. Those who weren't married, like Tony and Joe, would stay with their families, be it parents or a relative, and pass the time spending down their earnings before returning to the union hall.

Seamen had strange relationships with women. They loved to whore   it was their passion. But if they had a girl back home, she was to remain true. This was to a certain extent because of the allotment checks. They risked their lives and worked sixteen hours a day seven days a week for slave wages and felt resentful of their dependents, who were getting a free ride.

Marriage was a singular phenomenon. More often than not it happened overnight. Both Jake and the Bosun had tied the knot after having met a girl in a foreign country (Jake in Italy, Dave in South America) and fallen madly in love. Then they'd send for her from the States and she'd arrive after long and tedious State Department and immigration hassles. Rarely if ever were the matches made in heaven, though, and they soon turned into contracts of domestic convenience. The girls were also generally using matrimony as a means to emigrate.

So the sailors were a melancholy lot. Half their lives were spent either at sea or in godforsaken spots like Dumai. At home there was nothing to make them stay; a seaman writes himself out of any domestic security after only a year or so. Before long he knows no other life, has no other skills and no other future. Some advance through the ranks and become officers. Most are content to stay as ABs or QMEDs, not wishing to complicate what little stability there is left to their lives.

There was no hint of homosexuality on board. Occasionally you'd hear of a character or two, but that was rare. In Japan the sight of a woman was enough to give one the jitters. I felt like a Shaker when I first got ashore, the spasms literally running from my head to my toes and back. The officers were probably a different story. If they weren't gay, as the joke went, they were eunuchs.

The Bos and the chief mate hovered over me at this morning's OT while I was sugieing. Aye, it got on my nerves. Billy and all talk of boycott, but what the fuck, I need the money.

The saddest thing I've seen all trip are the storm-blown swallows and other birds who circle our ship expectantly and futilely pecking on our deck for food.

In these manic last daze you don't want to stir any waves if at all possible unless you can hold your own. If you don't real-

*ize what you're doing, that's okay, that's ignorance. But if you
do and you step on someone's toes, that's guilt.*

And so it goes.

—9/10/80

Entropy set in, settling over everyone on board the SS *Rose
City*. I stopped working in the morning, turning to only for
afternoon overtime. Billy continued to play dead for the mates
but found plenty of time to party.

There was one outstanding celebration, on the night of
Thursday the eleventh. Billy, Spider, Pete, Charlie, and I gathered forces in Ned's room. I had lent Billy my box while he was
recovering, so he brought that along to listen to his Frank Sina-
tra tapes. Billy didn't like rock and roll; he liked the crooners.

The six of us raged on uninhibitedly. Tony made a special
guest appearance and stole the show. He did his trick with the
cigar, making it disappear in his mouth and bringing it out
again and again until it was piping hot. That was when he swallowed it. The boys were so amazed they insisted he repeat the
performance three more times, with cigarettes. He received a
standing ovation.

Billy decided to return to work; he was sick of being sick.
However, the Chief wouldn't let him, consulting with the Second in secret. Billy drove his point home, though, and got his
way.

This issue settled, the Chief and the Old Man created a new
controversy by refusing to sell the crew any more of the beer we
had broken our backs loading in Japan. I asked the Chief what
the beef was. He rolled his eyes.

"Are you kidding, with the performers we got on this ship?"

I shrugged. We had a week or so to go and this guy was still looking for a way to regain the manhood he lost to the Bosun on the deck in Osaka Harbor. Miguel and Charlie were able to keep us supplied for a few days, but it wasn't enough. We had gone through Ned's thirty cases in a week, and we needed more.

Billy did the weekend's work with no trouble. He said nothing to the Chief, and the Chief said nothing to him. In the meantime we had passed through the Mariana Islands, over the Mariana Trench, and past a silent, dark Asunción Island.

Monday morning things returned to normal. The Chief called Jake and me up to the wheelhouse while we were on standby and had us give the bridge a complete cleaning. We were used to his new game of making us go out on lookout the instant the sun set and not knocking us off at dawn until the sun was fully risen, but this was ridiculous. He had calculated correctly, however. Billy and Jake started to bitch and swear. They accused the Chief of harassment.

The Chief smiled sarcastically and with a condescending pout replied, "Oh, is that so? Well, that's too bad."

Billy lost it and started screaming at the mate. The Chief had been waiting for this and immediately knocked Billy off watch, a bad new black mark in the log.

When Jake and I finished, I took over the wheel and Jake went down to Billy's room, where the two of them planned a "tragic relapse." As soon as I was relieved, they had me wake the Second again and tell him of Billy's condition. It was an Oscar-worthy performance. Jake stood by Billy's bed, holding his hand and shaking his head. Billy looked as though he were

THE VOYAGE OF THE ROSE CITY | 221

at death's door, so weak and pale was he. I thought I heard violins and a woman's voice cry out "Tara!"

Petty bullshit on a ship overwhelms. Bud is completely alienated by all.

Well, the Bos called a special meeting reprimanding us over the noise last night. Hypocrites. To think they never did it. I skipped it. Fuck that.

Found a mangled bird (in various pieces) by the door to the forepeak next to the carcass of a humongous beetle, two inches long. A few days before on the flying bridge I found an odd amalgam of fleshy remains, including tiny fish embedded in it. Today I saw the shriveled remains of a flying fish. So be it.

—9/12/80

Ten daze. Been getting too much shit from the old-timers.

—9/13/80

The Chief's pissed off because no one is working overtime this week. The reason for this is that instead of allowing us to project our work for the last few daze they wanted us to hand in our OT sheets plus next week's guaranteed, and work on a supplementary work ticket. Taxes and delays. Also, they want to hold us for the coming Coast Guard inspection. Well, we've all refused. They tried to get the other departments to do it, but they also refused.

—9/15/80

We were, in effect, on strike. Things had reached the point where it didn't matter how much money we might lose; we wanted to make the officers look bad. Tony and I were asked to stop all but required work, and we complied. The Bosun and the Chief had a long talk about this, but from what I could tell, Dave paled. Maybe he was keeping his cool because of Billy and Ned, who were both in serious trouble with the Coast Guard, but it could also have been that he didn't have it in him anymore. He was such a great guy, always there with a smile and a song, but I'd come across him sitting alone in the mess, breaking his diet in the middle of the night.

The other old-timers were becoming seriously tedious. I had long since taken to eating at the boys' table, and during the idle hours we would sit in the lounge while they hung out in the mess. Charlie called them a bunch of old hens, the way they cackled. The stories that were so amazing the first time around were excruciating by the fifth telling. It was as if they spoke through a phonograph that kept playing the same record over and over. You could predict when a certain episode was going to be told by the one that came before it.

Jake, in particular, was acting like a bedbug. Even the old-timers noticed the change. He darted around the house talking to himself and had a wounded-animal look in his eye. We called him "The Little Red Rooster," after the old blues tune. What his problem was we could only guess, but it certainly needed curing—there was no question about that.

On Tuesday the sixteenth we crossed the date line and returned in an abstraction to the world of Monday the fifteenth. I got a kick out of this, and the clocks advanced an hour. And before I could say "That's deeper than whale shit," the company handed us a surprise: We were going to be paid only once for Tuesday the sixteenth.

It didn't matter that, because of the date line, we had had two Tuesday the sixteenths; according to the calendar and the books, only one day came at a time, and so we would be paid only for Tuesday the sixteenth. It's a wonderful life.

Time passed and the confinement was increasingly hard to take. Tony invited me to stay with him for a few days at his home near Seattle. I accepted heartily and made plans to take off from there, traveling down the West Coast and over to New Orleans by train. It was pipe dreams like this that kept the mind from suffocating.

The third mate took over for the Chief on watch one afternoon. At first I'd thought he was a jerk, but over the months he turned out to be a decent guy. Like Joe, he had never bothered to upgrade. He liked having only a minimum of responsibility.

It was a quiet day and we were still headed in a straight line for Puget Sound. The Third turned to me: "I don't want to blow steam up your ass or anything, but you've done a hell of a job."

I was very startled by this. I thanked him with a silent nod as we went on.

"You don't cop an attitude of 'This is my first trip, so fuck it, etc. . . . ' And don't let those assholes down below get to you."

I then realized how little he really knew about life before the mast. I hadn't any choice but to perform to the best of my abilities. They would have kicked my head open if I hadn't. Not only that—his arrogance toward the crew was unacceptable.

The next morning he and the third engineer came up on the bridge drunk out of their minds. The Third leaned over the console. "Don't let those assholes down there influence you. They're all a bunch of derelicts." His eyes were bloodier than the new morning sun.

The Chief took over for him and covered it all up. But heaven forbid if a crewman was unable to function due to intoxication.

Channel fever. There were only two days to go, and we had to have a drink. Billy and Ned decided on a great plan: While the third engineer was on watch, we would sneak into his room and steal his beer.

We returned after a few minutes with a six-pack. We drank it, but it wasn't enough. We looked at one another and knew we had to get more.

The third mate was on watch. He lived on D deck with the rest of the deck officers. One floor below were the officers' lounge and the engineers' cabins. Above was the bridge.

We climbed like three ninjas up the outside staircase. Billy stood lookout in the inside stairwell, while I covered the back. Ned's job was the tough one: He had to sneak down the hall, slip into the third mate's room, and fill a garbage bag full of beer. There was only one hitch: The Old Man was up at his desk, typing, with his door open, only fifteen feet away. No matter—we wanted beer, and we wanted it now.

Ned crept down the hall and noiselessly opened the door and closed it behind him. I could hear the Captain's typewriter clacking away. Ned was staying in there a long time. Too long.

The Old Man stopped typing and grunted. I froze and listened to my heart thundering. He started typing again but there was still no sign of Ned. Billy slipped down the hall and was about to investigate when Ned emerged with a king's ransom. We took off out the back door and down the outside stairway. Billy burst in on C deck by mistake and we panicked. I leaped over the railing and slid down a pipe and into a hatch that led to the engine room. The feats of prowess one can perform when scared are tremendous.

I waited ten minutes before going to Ned's room. I knocked and Billy unlocked the door. It was incredible. Ned had stolen dozens of cold beers. He explained the delay by saying that when he opened the refrigerator and saw it filled with nothing else he stood in awe for a minute and a half. He wanted to take the whole thing.

We drank into the wee hours. They were the best beers I've ever tasted.

The last night the steward finally rounded up a poker game. A table was set up in the lounge, and as people came off watch the crew sat in. The steward was the master. He flipped the cards and made the right bets with great élan. But everyone at this game was as smooth as 007. They knew all the lingo. They slid their cards to the edge of the table and barely cracked them to see what hand they had. No one thought twice about losing two hundred dollars in a hand. This was real poker, and they were out to play.

I watched.

Five hours later we entered Puget Sound. Jake worked the wheel for the first hour, but eventually someone had to relieve him, and that somebody was me. I came onto the bridge just as we passed into the Sound proper. The Old Man was due up at any minute and the Chief warned me that it would be touch and go: It was foggy, there was a lot of traffic, and we were sailing with a pilot—he had boarded earlier—who kept a close eye on things. He also told me to repeat the commands as I executed them.

The bridge was tense. The only light came from the broken radar and the compass. The Old Man arrived wearing his uniform and his master's hat. He grunted and had the Chief fill him in. There was a new light on the bridge now: the Captain's cigar. The Old Man took position with his binoculars at the front of the bridge and peered out the window.

"Ten degrees right!"

I followed through in silence. The Chief poked me, and I remembered: "Ten degrees right." The ship moved ominously to the right, and I jerked the wheel twenty degrees left and stopped the momentum. In a moment she was straightened out on the new course. There was no margin for error.

"Five degrees left!"

"Five degrees left."

This continued for half an hour, until the radio barked we were headed for fishing nets and had to move fast. The Old Man couldn't wait for the pilot to plot a new course and had to improvise on the spot. He barked out a new order. I followed up and he shouted another. It went back and forth as we shifted course midway up the strait and weaved in and out of ships and sandbars.

We had made it with no problems. The Old Man got her on a new course and told me I could put her on auto for a while and take a cigarette break. Jake came up and took over. I had passed my final exam.

I sat down on a couch in the lounge. We were back. Dawn was rising and we could see the States out the starboard windows. I lit up a Djarum and inhaled deeply. It was all over. We could go home now.

My God.

THE OLYMPIC MOUNTAINS that surround the town of Port
Angeles rise from the edge of the Sound in a series of sheer
cliffs bathed in floating mists. It had been 103 days since we'd
seen America. Throughout the ship there was relief. After helping the company executives climb aboard from the launch, I
waited in the lounge for my mail. An hour later the Bosun
handed me a packet of letters and I ran eagerly up to my room
to read them.

In the corridor of B deck I came across Charlie and Billy.
Billy was staring out the window, clutching a letter and saying
nothing. Charlie put an arm around him.

"Hey, what can you do?" Charlie said in a low, compassion-
ate voice. "From the sound of it she was going to leave sometime. No marriage can last forever."

I slipped by them silently and closed the door to my room.
Poor Billy; what a hell of a welcome home.

That night I had a dream.

I am outside on the stern of the *Rose City*. It is night and the
wind howls with a desperate urgency. Billy is with me, and we
start running.

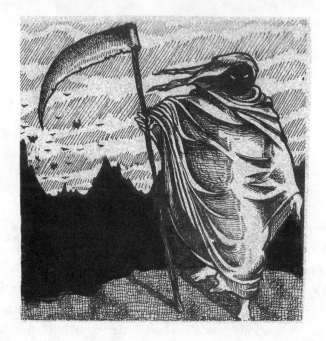

In a storeroom are dozens of six-foot-long wooden boxes. Billy and I start grabbing them and throwing them off the stern and into the water. Each time I run back to the storeroom I pause. The Voices have returned. They call from out on the bow, this awesome power. I face the wind and stare at the bow. If I leave the well-lit stern and go down the dark deck to the forepeak I will have it. The Voices promise—not nirvana, exactly, but some great awareness, a psychic perception. Perhaps even omniscience. In the gales, on the bow, in the dark they call, but I am too scared to go.

Billy and I keep tossing the boxes into the water. I could have IT if only I brave the walk to the bow. But I hesitate, afraid.

Then Billy is gone. I'm outside, on land. I fall to my knees and start digging, searching desperately. I have a mental image of a dead man's hand sticking up out of the earth, and I must find the body.

Then I wake up.

I didn't remember falling asleep. I was still fully dressed and all the lights in my room were on. I shivered and realized I was covered with a cold sweat.

Just then the Second, followed by Joe, entered my cabin through the bathroom door. Joe poked the Second. "You see, Mate? I told you he was asleep in his room."

They looked at me nervously.

"Are you all right?" the Second asked.

I stared at them, confused, still shaken from the dream.

"We just got a report that you were drowned. The Coast Guard is dragging the river for your body."

I stared uncomprehendingly at the two of them. "What are you talking about?"

"The launch pilot just found Billy in the water, clinging to a pier. I guess he tried to kill himself. When the ambulance took him off to the hospital he was screaming, 'John Monahan is dead! He's drowned! He's dead. . . .' "

The room fell silent.

I sat up slowly. The two events, my dream and Billy's suicide attempt, corresponded exactly. Billy had been in the forty-degree water an hour before they pulled him out with a fishing lance. I shivered at what might have happened if I had had the courage to meet the Voices on the bow.

In a shaky voice I told the two of them about the dream.

Again the room fell silent. Eventually a stunned Joe spoke up: "That's fucking . . . why that's fucking psychiatric!"

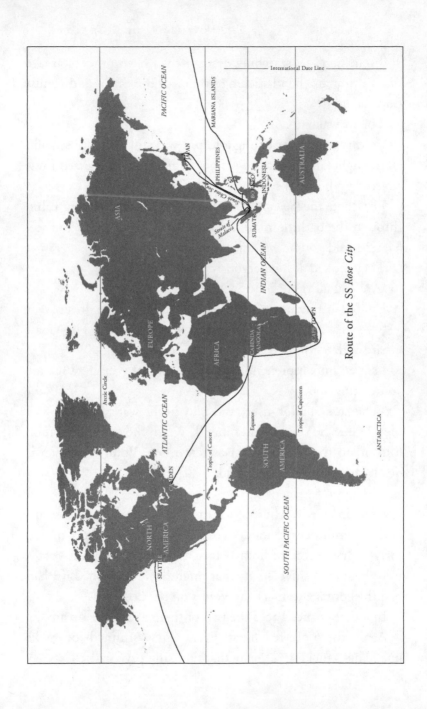

Route of the SS *Rose City*

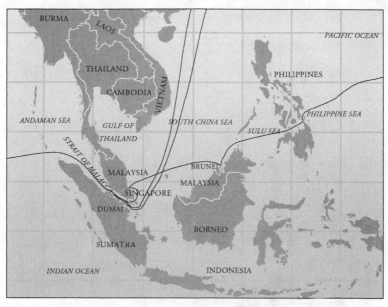

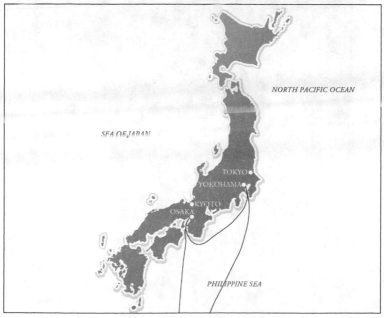

YOUNG MAN AT SEA

A Note from Elizabeth Moynihan

John McCloskey Moynihan was born during a blizzard in Syracuse, New York, on February 15, 1960. He was named for an exceptional person, Mark McCloskey, familiarly called Grandpa Mac by our three children. When he was a child John's favorite food was bread, his favorite comic strip was *The Phantom,* and his favorite hat was a deerstalker.

After kindergarten at John Eaton School in Washington, D.C., John spent one tumultuous week at P.S. 113 in New York City before arriving at Central School in Middletown, Connecticut. He endured another move and six dreary weeks at the Agassi School before transferring to six happy years at Buckingham School in Cambridge, Massachusetts. He spent two amazing years at the American International School in New Delhi, returned to Cambridge for one semester at Browne and Nichols, then went on to high school at Phillips Academy, Andover. On his first call home from Wesleyan University he said he was blown away because in his class he had met someone from every school he'd ever attended.

After Wesleyan he worked on the *Boston Herald* but decided not to pursue a career in journalism; instead he moved to New York, earned his M.F.A. at the Tisch School at NYU, and became a freelance animator. He considered moving to Los Angeles but found it hard to leave New York, though he loved traveling the world, which he did frequently, usually by unconventional means.

John was blessed with enormous talent, intellectual curiosity, a creative sense of humor, and many friends. Although his marriage ended in divorce and he had no children, he was beloved by his nephew, Mikey, and Zora, his niece. They called him Uncle Black Jack and loved his pirate games—a name and games quickly adopted by his friends' children as well. He was always creating scenarios and drew his close friends and family into the game he made of life. He was a prolific letter writer and could compose an entire short story on a postcard.

John was a generous and sympathetic person, and his life and career had exciting highs and steep lows, but in his last few years he found his ideal anchorage in Sydney, Australia. He had finally cracked the immigration code and was awaiting his resident visa when he died suddenly on October 15, 2004. He had hoped to be in Sydney by Christmas, so on December 20, 2004, his dear friend Steed Hinckley and I, accompanied by a wonderful group of John's Australian friends—or mates, as he called them—sailed to a cove he knew well on the edge of Sydney Harbor. At 151°E by 34°S we released his ashes on the gentle waves, his last voyage.

He is sorely missed.

A Word about the Ship

Launched in 1976 as a supertanker in the San Clemente class, in 1987 the SS *Rose City* was converted to a hospital ship for the U.S. Navy, and is now called the USNS *Comfort*. The original cathedral-sized tanks now hold twelve fully equipped operating rooms, a one-thousand-bed hospital facility, and all necessary laboratory and technical support systems. Its primary mission is to provide flexible rapid medical and surgical care for U.S. military forces, and its secondary mission is for relief and humanitarian efforts worldwide. With a crew of sixty-seven civil service mariners, the *Comfort* arrived in Haiti on January 20, 2010, and the 560 medical and 110 support personnel immediately began treating earthquake victims. John McCloskey Moynihan, Ordinary Seaman, would be thrilled by the ship's transformation and mission.

ABOUT THE TYPE

This book was set in Garamond, a typeface originally designed by the Parisian typecutter Claude Garamond (1480–1561). This version of Garamond was modeled on a 1592 specimen sheet from the Egenolff-Berner foundry, which was produced from types assumed to have been brought to Frankfurt by the punchcutter Jacques Sabon.

Claude Garamond's distinguished romans and italics first appeared in *Opera Ciceronis* in 1543–44. The Garamond types are clear, open, and elegant.